OBSERVATIONS DURING A TOUR TO THE LAKES

Chapter House, Furness Abbey, by T. Allom, 1845

OBSERVATIONS
DURING A TOUR TO THE LAKES
of ## LANCASHIRE, WESTMORELAND, AND CUMBERLAND

by
ANN RADCLIFFE

EDITED AND INTRODUCED
by
PENNY BRADSHAW

SECOND EDITION

THE HOBNOB PRESS

For Larry and Alex, with love

First published by Bookcase in 2014

This second edition published in the United Kingdom in 2024
by The Hobnob Press,
8 Lock Warehouse, Severn Road, Gloucester GL1 2GA
www.hobnobpress.co.uk

British Library Cataloguing in Publication Data
A catalogue record for this book is available from the British Library

ISBN 978-1-914407-64-2 hardback
ISBN 978-1-914407-65-9 paperback

Typeset in Adobe Garamond Pro 11/14 pt.
Typesetting and origination by John Chandler

CONTENTS

PREFACE TO THE SECOND EDITION

T HE FIRST EDITION of this edited volume of Ann Radcliffe's *Observations during a Tour to the Lakes of Lancashire, Westmoreland, and Cumberland* was published in 2014 by Bookcase. This, the only modern critical edition of any part of Radcliffe's 1795 travel-text to have been published, is now out of print and so I am delighted to have been given the opportunity to bring out a second edition with Hobnob Press in the 10th anniversary year of that original publication.

The design and layout of this second edition of *Observations* are new but my critical 'Introduction' and editorial notes are reproduced here as they appear in the first edition.

I remain extremely grateful to Steve Matthews at Bookcase for bringing out the first edition of this volume back in 2014, and I would like to thank Dr John Chandler and Dr Louise Ryland-Epton of Hobnob Press for their support and enthusiasm for this 10th anniversary edition, which will ensure that a modern critical edition of Radcliffe's important and influential piece of Romantic-era Lake District travel writing continues to be readily available to readers and scholars.

Dr Penny Bradshaw
Ambleside,
January 2024

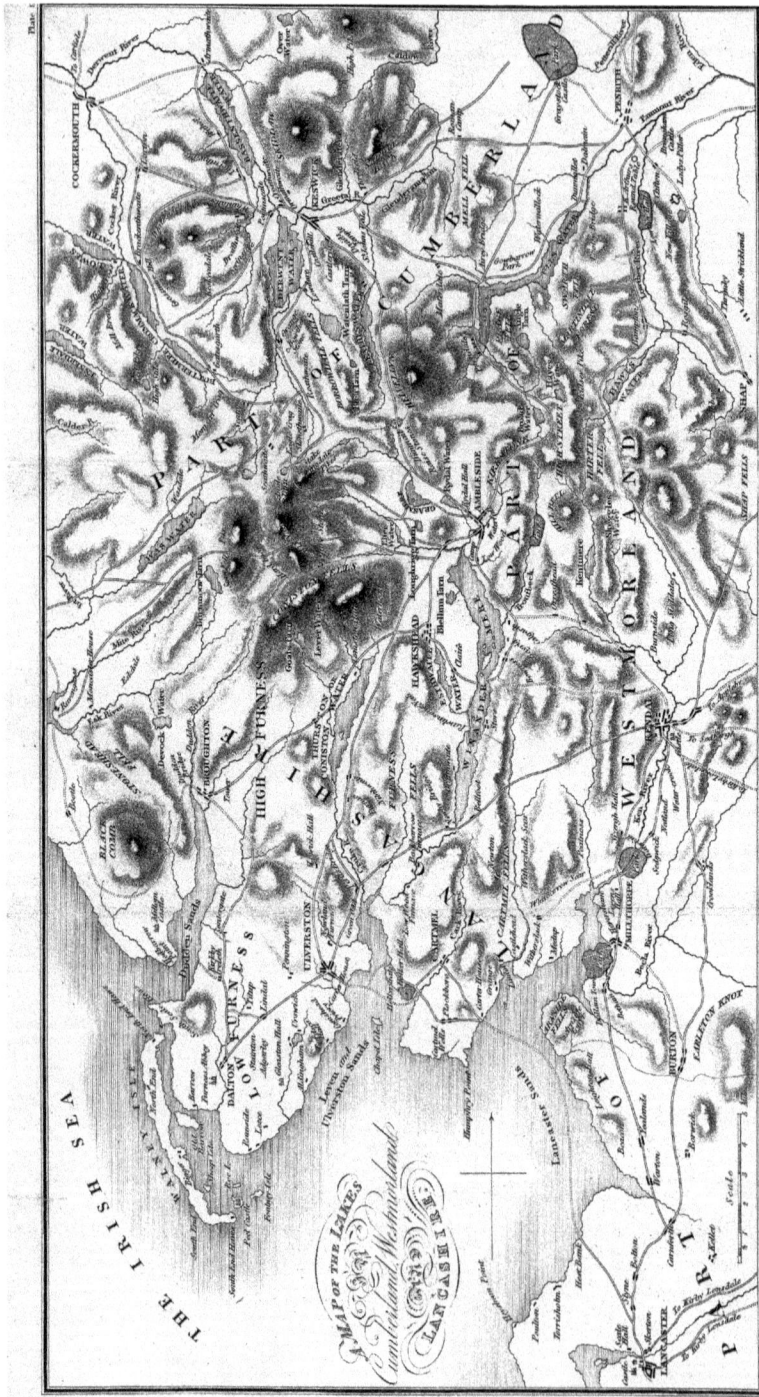

Map of the Lakes included in the 3rd edition of *Thomas West's Guide to the Lakes, 1784*

INTRODUCTION

IN THE AUTUMN of 1794, Ann Radcliffe, one of the best known and most popular novelists of the late eighteenth-century, set off on a tour of the Lake District with her husband. She was at the very height of her fame, having already published three of her most successful novels, *A Sicilian Romance, The Romance of the Forest,* and *The Mysteries of Udolpho* in 1790, 1791, and 1794 respectively. During the visit she kept a journal and the following year she published her account of the tour as *Observations during a Tour to the Lakes of Lancashire, Westmoreland, and Cumberland.*[1] This text would contribute to the evolution of ideas about the Lakes landscape during the period in which that region was opening up as a site of aesthetic and cultural significance, and when the Wordsworthian response to the Lakes had yet to be developed. Along with the presence of Wordsworth, Thomas De Quincey points to Radcliffe's account as the most significant literary influence shaping his own interest in the region prior to his moving there in 1809 and in 1818 Keats would also refer to Radcliffe's tour during the preparations for his own journey North. Despite the importance of the text within Romantic contexts, *Observations* has subsequently been marginalised in a textual history of the Lakes which tends to move all too simplistically from the early picturesque travel guides to Wordsworth's transformatory construction of an anti-picturesque poetics of place from 1799 onwards, following his taking up residence in Grasmere. The journey from Thomas West's *A Guide to the Lakes* (1778) to Wordsworth, or from the picturesque to Romanticism is, however, much more complex than such narratives would suggest and, if we are to unravel this process of transition, more needs to be done in terms of mapping what took place *between* these dates in terms of literary responses to the Lakes. Ann Radcliffe, along with other Romantic-era women writers, came to the Lakes in the wake of Gray and West, and published their own creative constructions of this place, constructions which are long overdue a reconsideration.[2] As the foremost Gothic novelist of her generation, Radcliffe brings a writer's imagination and her passion for the Gothic to bear on her experience of the Lakes, offering us a fascinatingly unfamiliar and, at times, experimental account of this landscape and its meanings. She also though begins to move us towards the more politicised account of the Lakes which would subsequently come to be identified with Wordsworth, in her recognition that within this region a certain independence of spirit combined with remoteness from the corruptions of the urban had created a refuge for the ideals of liberty.

Mrs Radcliffe - 'the Mighty Enchantress'

T HOUGH RADCLIFFE'S TOUR has been all but written out of narratives about the cultural development of the Lakes, she is the most important and significant writer to visit the Lake District and write about her experiences here in the early part of the Romantic period, and – unlike Wordsworth – she comes to the region at a point in her career when her reputation and identity as a writer had been clearly established. Radcliffe's fame rested on her pioneering development of the Gothic novel which had rendered that style of fiction the staple of middle-class entertainment and she was, as her most recent biographer notes, the 'best-paid novelist of her generation'.[3] Her style was so distinctive that the name 'Mrs Radcliffe' became synonymous with certain kinds of Gothic landscapes, plots, characters, and emotional lexicon. At the point of her death in 1823 there was a clear recognition that she had made a unique contribution to English literature with her Gothic romances, which were deemed 'a class apart from all which had gone before'.[4] Sir Walter Scott refers to her as the 'mighty enchantress' and identifies her as the 'founder of a class, or school' of literature and as having 'led the way in a peculiar style of composition, affecting powerfully the mind of the reader, which has since been attempted by many, but in which no one has attained or approached the excellencies of the original inventor'.[5] The author of Radcliffe's first official memoir notes that she may 'fairly be considered as the inventor of a new style of romance; equally distinct from the old tales of chivalry and magic, and from modern representations of credible incidents and living manners....She occupied that middle region between the mighty dreams of the heroic ages and the realities of our own, which remained to be possessed' (Talfourd, p. 67).

Radcliffe's fame and popularity notwithstanding, her personal story is an intriguing one and while we can map the domestic lives of many of the writers associated with the Lakes in close detail through an abundance of letters and journals, there is a significant dearth of information about one of the most famous and widely read female writers of the period.[6] Perhaps one of the best known literary anecdotes about Radcliffe is that in 1882 the Victorian poet Christina Rossetti undertook to write a biography of the late novelist, but had to give the project up because of lack of information, especially regarding the details of her final years. For early information about her life, contemporary biographers are still forced to rely primarily on two main sources. The first of these is an obituary of 1824 which incorporates a letter containing details from an unnamed source who provides 'authentic' personal information and who was, in all likelihood, Radcliffe's widower, William.[7] The second key authoritative source is the subsequent 'Memoir of the Life and Writings of Mrs. Radcliffe' of 1826. The 'Memoir' was published anonymously and was initially and incorrectly attributed to her husband. It was in fact written by Sir Thomas Noon Talfourd, a lawyer, reviewer and writer. Talfourd was also a friend of Wordsworth, Coleridge, and the Lambs, who knew William Radcliffe through shared legal and journalistic circles. Talfourd's was the official Radcliffe biography and he certainly had access to some of Radcliffe's journals and to private family information. Talfourd later acknowledged though that William Radcliffe's close involvement in writing the authorised memoir was in fact a major hindrance, observing that 'the trouble of drawing up this life, under the jealous supervision of Mr Radcliffe, exceeds anything that can be imagined'.[8] Though less important as a biographical source, a third significant early reflection on her life work was offered by the novelist Sir Walter Scott, in his 'Prefatory Memoir to Mrs Ann Radcliffe', which was prefixed to a complete one volume edition of Radcliffe's novels published by the Edinburgh press of James Ballantyne in 1824.

Based on both early and late biographical information there seems little dispute regarding the main facts about her early life. Radcliffe was born Ann Ward in London in 1764 to respectable and comfortably off parents. Her father, William Ward, was in the haberdashery business and thus firmly situated within the burgeoning middle-class but her mother, Ann Oates, had more interesting and promising connections. Her mother's cousin was physician to George III and her brother-in-law was Josiah Wedgwood's business partner and, as a result of these maternal connections, the Ward family moved to Bath, thus giving the young Ann better opportunities to socialise and meet literary figures of the day. No authorised visual representation of Radcliffe exists, but within the letter which was incorporated in the 1824 obituary the following pen-portrait is offered: 'This admirable writer, whom I remember from about the time of her twentieth year, was, in her youth, of a figure exquisitely proportioned....Her complexion was beautiful, as was her whole countenance, especially her eyes, eyebrows and mouth' (cited in 'Mrs Ann Radcliffe', p. 99). This letter also identifies an early love of natural landscapes in the young Ann Ward and suggests that one of her 'chief delights' was 'To contemplate the glories of creation, but more particularly the grander features of their display' (*ibid.*).

In 1787, at the age of 23, Ann Ward married William Radcliffe, an Oxford law graduate and journalist, who became the part-owner and editor of a paper called the *English Chronicle*. Though childless, the marriage seems to have been on the whole a happy one and Radcliffe refers to him quite touchingly in the preface to the 1795 tour as her 'nearest relative and friend' (*Journey*, p. v). After the marriage the young couple moved to London where William was often obliged to work long and late hours running his paper. Radcliffe began writing during the lonely evenings of her early married life, initially to alleviate her boredom, 'beguil[ing] the else weary hours by her pen' and reading out the results to her husband when he finally returned from work (Talfourd, p. 6). William Radcliffe certainly seems to have encouraged his wife's literary talents and just two years after the marriage her first short novel was published: *The Castles of Athlin and Dunbayne. A Highland Story* (1789). Though Radcliffe is better known for her fictional portrayal of Continental landscapes, this first text is set in Scotland and draws on those dramatic Scottish landscapes which bear a marked similarity with those she would explore in her later tour of the North of England.

The following year Radcliffe published a second and more substantial novel, *A Sicilian Romance* (1790), which would really begin to establish the Radcliffean style. It was her first major success and Scott recalls that it 'attracted in no ordinary degree the attention of the public' (Scott, p. iv). This was followed hard on the heels by *The Romance of the Forest* (1791) with which she achieved both national and international fame, and widespread critical acclaim. The pinnacle of Radcliffe's success came, however, with the next novel, *The Mysteries of Udolpho* (1794), a book which has never been out of print and which would secure her a place in the literary canons of the future even after the Gothic novel and its trappings had long gone out of fashion. As Bonamy Dobrée notes, for 'some years after its publication in 1794' this novel was '"required reading" for anybody who had any pretence at all to being a person of education, or culture, or even of popular reading habits'.[9] It was in the year in which *Udolpho* was published, and using the first instalment of the royalties from that book, that Ann Radcliffe and her husband set out on a tour of the Continent in order to explore the sorts of scenery which her novels describe, but which Radcliffe had not at that point encountered in person. The Continental part of the tour ended up being curtailed and failed to fulfil Radcliffe's expectations but, on returning to England, the Radcliffes set forth on an alternative expedition to the English Lakes. In 1795 Radcliffe published her experiences of these travels as *A Journey Made in the Summer of 1794, through Holland and the Western Frontier of Germany, with a Return down the Rhine: to which are Observations during added a Tour to the Lakes of Lancashire, Westmoreland, and Cumberland*. It was the first and only piece of travel writing which she would publish during her lifetime. Two years later, Radcliffe published *The Italian* (1797), a text which prompted one critic to refer to her as the 'Shakespeare of Romance Writers'.[10] Radcliffe's popularity with her reading public had never been greater but quite suddenly, at the age of 33, Radcliffe stopped publishing. She would live for another 26 years but no further publications appeared during her lifetime and very few details about her private life would emerge during this period. As Walter Scott observes in his 'Prefatory Memoir', 'it was from no coldness on the part of the public, that, like an actress in full possession of applauded powers, she chose to retreat from the stage in the blaze of her fame....We are left in vain to conjecture the reason' (xv).

As Scott goes on to record, in the absence of facts, the contemporary public began to invent their own Radcliffean version of events:

> many of her admirers believed, and some are not yet undeceived, that, in consequence of brooding over the terrors which she depicted, her reason had at length been overturned, and that the author of *The Mysteries of Udolpho* only existed as the melancholy inmate of a private mad-house. This report was so generally spread, and so confidently repeated in print, as well as in conversation, that the Editor believed it for several years, until, greatly to his satisfaction, he learned from good authority that there neither was, nor ever had been, the most distant foundation for this unpleasing rumour (Scott, p. xvii).

Though Radcliffe's early biographers were at pains to deny these lurid speculations, most continued to remark on the extreme privacy and secrecy in which she had lived her life. As one reviewer observed, 'She never appeared in public, nor mingled in private society, but kept herself apart, like the sweet bird that sings its solitary notes, shrouded and unseen'.[11] Scott himself acknowledged that she 'appears to have been as retired and sequestered, as the fame of her writings was brilliant and universal' and observes that 'no author, whose works were so universally read and admired, was so little personally known' (p. i and p. xvi).

Though some light was shed posthumously on her later life, curiosity about the reasons behind her abandonment of the Gothic novel created a great deal of speculation both then and now. Most critics have tended to relate her retreat from publishing to personal anxieties about the increasing tide of criticism which was mounting against Gothic fiction – a genre which she herself had done so much to define and develop, and to which her own name was irrevocably associated. Scott suggests that she 'may have been disgusted at seeing the mode of composition, which she had brought into fashion, prophaned by the host of servile imitators, who could only copy and render more prominent her defects, without aspiring to her merits' (xvi). Indeed in recent critical contexts her final novel, *The Italian*, has been read as in part a response to the revulsion against the new directions Gothic fiction was taking in texts such as *The Monk* (1796), a notorious novel by Matthew Lewis which, in its disturbing treatment of rape and murder, did much to bring about the backlash in public feeling towards the genre as a whole. By 1797, the year in which Radcliffe's final novel was published, a critique of the cultural frenzy for 'horrid novels' had certainly begun to be apparent; the popularity of such texts was seen by many to indicate a degradation of the public taste and became connected to fears about those emotional excesses which were perceived to have shaped the terrible events recently witnessed over the channel in France during the Revolutionary turmoil.

Radcliffe did in fact make one further tentative intervention in the field of novel-writing, with a historical romance, entitled *Gaston de Blondeville*. This was written in 1802 but only appeared in print posthumously in 1826 and, according to Talfourd, had not been intended for publication. It is to this posthumously published novel that Talfourd's memoir is prefixed. What is of far more interest though than the novel itself, which most critics agree is a poor conclusion to her career as a novelist, are the extracts from Radcliffe's private travel journals which were included within the memoir. Talfourd incorporates these by way of presenting evidence to refute the rumours that Radcliffe had 'sunk into a state of mental alienation' (p. 60) in the final years of her life. As these journals clearly demonstrate, far from languishing in a life of mentally disturbed seclusion for over two decades, Radcliffe had in fact entered into a new and deeply fulfilling lifestyle. Following the publication of *The Italian* in 1797 and up to and including 1812, she took bi-annual tours with her husband and wrote privately but extensively about these travel experiences. In the absence of any other autobiographical writing, Talfourd turns to these travel journals as a means of exploring Radcliffe's private thoughts during these years, noting that 'the means of watching the development of her faculties and tastes in her daily pursuits are supplied by copious memorandums written on several of her journies' (p. 4). It may well be that anxieties about the Gothic mode made Radcliffe perceive these private journal reflections on place and landscape as a safer and less problematic outlet for her creative talents. Talfourd reminds the reader that these expeditions were funded by her earlier unprecedented success as a writer, noting that her 'pecuniary resources' were now 'ample', but this financial comfort may also have reduced her inclination to produce any more fiction along the formulaic lines she had herself designed. Examining these journals alongside the published tour of 1795 suggests too that her explorations of *real* landscapes may have had an unexpected consequence on her attitudes toward the Gothic novel, in challenging the aesthetic ideals of the picturesque on which her novels had relied so extensively. These ideas will be explored in the later discussion of *Observations* but such a reading might lead us to conclude that her 1795 tour, far from being peripheral within Radcliffe's oeuvre, is rather at the very heart of the greatest mystery regarding her life.

The asthmatic condition which plagued Radcliffe's latter years seems to have set in somewhere around 1812 and meant that less regular excursions were possible thereafter but, even after this date, travel and exploration of new landscapes continue to feature as an important element of her life-story. Talfourd includes an extract from a travel journal penned during a visit to Ramsgate in October 1822, which is one of her last known pieces of writing. In this, Radcliffe's rendering of the landscape shows an increasing attention to capturing the scene before her in as accurate a way as possible, recording the fine detail in a manner that recalls passages in the journals of Dorothy Wordsworth:

> Stormy day, rain without sun, except that early a narrow line of palest silver fell on the horizon, showing, here and there, distant vessels in their course. Ships riding in the Downs, exactly on the sea-line, over the entrance into the harbour, opposite to our windows, were but dim and almost shapeless hints of what they were.
>
> This harbour was not now, as some hours since, flooded with a silver light, but grey and dull, in quiet contrast with the foaming waves at its entrance. The horizon thickened, and the scene around seemed to close in; but the vessels as they approached, though darker, became more visible and distinct (cited in Talfourd, p. 64).

The passage indicates that after the publication of *Journey* Radcliffe continued to experiment with travel writing and that this new mode of discourse came to replace the Gothic style for which she was best known. Here the scene is revealed through close observation of the changes and shifts within a living landscape. Though viewed from a window, there is no sense of this providing a frame for an artificially fixed scene – rather she seems to move outside the frame and witness the full panorama of ever-changing light and colour. There is a juxtaposition of movement and stillness which reveals this to be a specific landscape existing within time and space. This passage clearly reveals that the seed of Radcliffe's passion of travel writing and for documenting real natural landscapes, which was planted during her 1794 tour of the Continent and the Lakes, remained with her to the end of her life.

Radcliffe died in February 1823, just four months after this passage was written, at the age of 58. Talfourd turns to the medical report from her physician, Dr Scudamore, for an official account of her death. Despite years of lurid speculations about her condition, he provides the prosaic explanation that Radcliffe's death had been the result of a rapid decline triggered by 'exposure to cold' during the winter months resulting in inflammation of the lungs, or pleurisy (p. 65).

Though Radcliffe's influence stretches into the nineteenth century and beyond through a line of writers which includes the Brontës and Dickens, the Gothic novel itself had fallen out of favour within her own lifetime and Radcliffe's fame and popularity went into a fairly rapid decline. In 1862 the Victorian novelist, W. H. Thackeray, reminiscing about her fading reputation, considered the irony of the fact that *Udolpho* – 'one of the most famous romances which ever was published in this country' – was unknown to the younger generation.[12] Perhaps even more ironically, the changing tide of popularity was to a large extent fuelled by those of her contemporaries in whose work we can trace complex lines of influence. The Lake Poets – and especially Wordsworth – played a key role in turning the tide of opinion against the Radcliffean Gothic mode and though Scott's 'Prefatory Memoir' acknowledged Radcliffe's contribution to the development of the late eighteenth-century novel, it was nonetheless a text in which, as Norton suggests, he 'had cleverly planted the seeds of his rival's downfall' and elsewhere Scott more overtly attacked the 'Radcliffe school', carefully distinguishing his own romances from this earlier body of work (p. 259). The silencing of Radcliffe's voice within the narrative of the development of Lakes literature has been particularly effective, and a great deal of work needs to be done in terms of writing her back into that narrative and exploring the complex ways in which her tour connects up vital developments in the transformation of responses to this region within the Romantic period.

The Landscapes of Radcliffe's Fiction

R ADCLIFFE'S TREATMENT of the Lakes landscape in *Observations* is partly
of course influenced by her identity as a Gothic novelist and shaped by
her quite sophisticated understanding of the expectations and tastes of her
readership. As the inventor of a new style of fiction, which was known for
specific tropes, scenery, plots, characters, and discourse, Radcliffe comes to
the Lakes with certain writerly perspectives. These lead her to develop new
ideas about a physical terrain which was still in the process of imaginative
discovery. Our understanding of Radcliffe's account of the Lakes can therefore
be enhanced by a prior consideration of the handling of landscape within her
Gothic novels and by an awareness of the main aesthetic and philosophical
influences shaping those fictional landscapes.

Though the first recognised Gothic novel was Hugh Walpole's *Castle of
Otranto* (1764), there was very little further development of this genre before
the appearance of Radcliffe's fiction in the late 1780s and 90s. Following the
success and popularity of the Radcliffean Gothic, however, the marketplace
rapidly became flooded with this type of fiction. Radcliffe – to borrow an
appropriate metaphor – fleshed out the bones of the skeletal framework which
Walpole had devised, giving life and interest to the story with sentimentally
drawn characters, romantic interludes, and emotional turbulence. A further
crucial ingredient which Radcliffe brings to the basic Gothic formula
established by Walpole is a detailed engagement with natural landscapes, and
an exploration of the effects of these landscapes on the mind and emotions of
her characters, especially her female protagonists. The focus on landscapes was
such a marked feature of Radcliffe's fiction that, when she turned her attention
to the Lake District in a piece of travel writing, critics perceived the step as a
natural transition, commenting on her 'strong turn and taste for landscape, or
the description of the external face of nature' which 'may be said....to be her
forte'.[13]

Indeed it is Radcliffe's incorporation of extended passages relating to
travel, journeying, and natural sublime scenery which helps partly to account
for the extreme popularity of her writing, since in weaving these elements into
her fiction she was responding to the apparently unquenchable fashion for travel
and tourism in the late eighteenth-century. Radcliffe's extensive depiction of
natural landscapes in her fiction should remind us that the development of
the Gothic novel was intimately linked to the rise in travel tourism, and to the
aesthetic and philosophical ideas underpinning such tourism in this period.
Radcliffe's handling of this material in her fiction assumes a readership deeply

interested in such subject matter, and she absorbs both the language of travel discourse and contemporary landscape aesthetics into her writing. Both the Gothic novel and the rise of tourism are influenced by a number of inter-related philosophical and aesthetic ideas, and Radcliffe's treatment of landscape both in her fiction and subsequently in her tour needs to be understood in relation to the development of these ideas.

One of the seminal influences on Radcliffe, as on the Romantic poets, was a new understanding of the emotional effects of certain landscapes, ideas which were proposed most powerfully by Edmund Burke in his 1757 philosophical treatise, *A Philosophical Enquiry into the Origin of our Ideas of the Sublime and Beautiful*. Burke argues that certain dark, mountainous, stormy landscapes, have the potential to engender a state of awe and terror:

> The passion caused by the great and sublime in *nature*, when those causes operate most powerfully, is Astonishment; and astonishment is that state of the soul, in which all of its motions are suspended, with some degree of horror. In this case the mind is so entirely filled with its object, that it cannot entertain any other, nor by consequence reason on the object which employs it.[14]

The experience generated by such 'sublime' landscapes is identified by Burke as one of the most intense emotions a human is capable of experiencing and Radcliffe, clearly fascinated by this idea, would draw extensively on the concept of the sublime in her fiction to explore the ways in which such landscapes affect her characters, especially her heroines. A repeated trope in her novels is for the heroine to be taken on journeys which involve encounters with sublime scenery and which trigger the Burkean experience, such as the 'majestic and sublime alps whose aspect fills the soul with emotions of indescribable awe, and seems to lift it to a noble nature'; in such landscapes the heroine's 'spirits' are 'gradually revived and elevated by the grandeur of the images' since 'objects seem to impart somewhat of their own force, their own sublimity to the soul'.[15] Sublime encounters and Burkean responses such as these recur repeatedly throughout her fiction and became a defining feature of the Radcliffean Gothic.

A second and related influence on Radcliffe is the aesthetic ideal of the picturesque which grew out of Burkean landscape categories; in the picturesque, Burke's category of the sublime and its opposing category, the beautiful, are combined in ideal landscapes. It was popular interest in the picturesque which fuelled the fashion for travel and travel literature in the

1770s and 80s, as travellers were directed in search of landscapes which conformed to picturesque criteria as established by figures such as William Gilpin and Thomas West. As picturesque tourism was predicated on the idea of viewing the actual landscape as if it were a picture, a Claude glass was often carried by the traveller and used to contain the scene and produce the correct effect.[16] Radcliffe was deeply interested in the landscape art which had influenced the rise of the picturesque and its related aesthetic categories of the sublime and the beautiful. Within her fiction she refers explicitly to the work of influential seventeenth-century landscape artists, Claude Lorrain, Salvator Rosa, and Nicolas Poussin on numerous occasions and often presents passages of landscape description to her reader's imagination by comparing it to a scene painted by these artists; we are told, for example, in *The Mysteries of Udolpho* that the scene faced by the heroine is one 'as *Salvator* would have chosen, had he then existed, for his canvas'.[17] Radcliffe's tendency to depict landscape scenes in her fiction as 'framed' by windows or arches also draws our attention to the influence of the picturesque, and landscape art more broadly, on her writing.

A third important influence on Radcliffe's handling of natural landscapes is the work of Jean-Jacques Rousseau whose ideas, as expressed in his novels *Julie: or the New Heloise* (1761) and *Emile, or On Education* (1762), would also play a significant role in the development of a Wordsworthian poetics. Rousseau argues for the importance of a close relationship with nature in the moral development of man and Radcliffe clearly adopts key elements of Rousseau's thinking in her own development of character, with her fiction exploring the moral influence of certain landscapes. All of her novels display clear traces of a Rousseauvian influence but she explores these ideas most explicitly in *The Romance of the Forest*. This novel offers a critique of the 'vicious pleasures of society' which 'deaden' the 'finest feelings' and taint the heart (*The Romance of the Forest*, p. 272), presenting us instead with a model-family who live a virtuous and simple life, and who respond powerfully to the beauties of the natural world.[18]

Radcliffe's fiction responds to all of these eighteenth-century philosophical and aesthetic ideas in a variety of ways, and her writing would serve to further popularise and disseminate developing ideas about the importance of our relationship with natural landscapes. Radcliffe's engagement with these ways of thinking in her fiction, is however, more interesting and complex than any simple identification of each separate influence and ingredient would suggest. While Radcliffe's treatment of landscape in her novels is certainly more formulaic and artificial than in her travel writing, even here she seems to be working with and processing these ideas, so that at times she introduces new dimensions to the function of landscape in literature. Both she and her close contemporary, Charlotte Smith, in making dramatic natural landscapes a central feature of their fiction, played a crucial role in invoking the idea of the role played by nature in shaping the morality of mankind and in showing the impact of the natural landscape on the mind of man and, more especially, on women.

One of the reasons why Radcliffe needs to be recognised as an important stepping stone in the journey towards Wordsworth and his landscape poetry is that, while fascinated by the visual arts and physical embodiments of the sublime and picturesque, she is also interested in mapping and exploring these ideas in language. Scott describes her fictional scenes as those 'which could only have been drawn by one to whom nature has given the eye of the painter, with the spirit of a poet' (p. vi) and he describes her as the 'first poetess of romantic fiction[.]' (p. iv). The identification of poetry as the natural form of expression for the emotional effects caused by the sublime in nature emerges in her very first novel, *The Castles of Athlin and Dunbayne,* a text which also establishes an early interest in the imaginative possibility of remote northern landscapes. Her hero, Osbert, is defined by his enthusiasm for these wild landscapes, to which he responds primarily through the language of poetry:

> His warm imagination directed him to poetry, and he followed where she led. He loved to wander among the Romantic scenes of the Highlands, where the wild variety of nature inspired him with all of the enthusiasm of his favourite art.[19]

This pattern is repeated in other Radcliffe fictions and often it is the heroine who has such poetic leanings or who is shown to be powerfully responsive to poetry. In *The Romance of the Forest,* Clara La Luc's Rousseauvian upbringing and delight in the 'observance of nature', result in her displaying 'a taste for poetry and painting'; the novel's heroine, Adeline, is also a poet and her delight at 'the surrounding scenery' inspires her writing: 'ye shadowy forms! attend my lonely hours, / Still chase my real cares with your illusive powers!' (*The Romance of the Forest,* p. 249).[20] Radcliffe's fiction further seeks to develop the link between poetic language and external landscapes by making constant references to English poetry, insisting on constructing her visual scenes and her reader's responses to them not only through the language of Burke and the visual art of Salvator Rosa and Claude Lorrain, but also through a complex patchwork of poets which includes Collins, Milton, and Shakespeare. This has the effect of situating the Gothic within a respectable English literary heritage, but it also identifies poetic language as the ideal way of representing the effects of such landscapes on the human mind.

If poetry is prioritised in Radcliffe's fiction, so too is the female perspective. Given that one of the predominant features of the Radcliffean Gothic is a focus on the emotional effects of external landscapes on the mind of the heroine, a complex relationship comes to be developed in her fiction between the female protagonist and these sublime natural landscapes. This development can itself be related to the rise of the fashionable discourse of sensibility, which encouraged the development of powerful emotional responsiveness in both men and women. As Robert Miles suggests:

> Sensibility declared a democracy of the heart, an egalitarian world of feelings where all were equal who wept before scenes of tragic benevolence, or who shuddered with delightful terror before sublime manifestations of the divine power. As such, sensibility constituted a language of equal emotional entitlements, a democracy of feeling hearts that greatly assisted women in defending their personal interests.[21]

While both male and female characters respond powerfully to the effects of particular landscapes in Radcliffe's fiction, it is predominantly her heroines who linger over such scenes and who appear to be most intensely affected by them.

Though the discourse of sensibility validates the idea of intense emotional experience for both sexes, the concept of the sublime has long been recognised as a gendered category, conforming to characteristics which have been culturally associated with masculinity, since Burke connects it with power, immensity, roughness, and vastness, but also to the divine presence of God. Consequently, the sublime has been described by later critics as being associated with 'an experience of masculine empowerment' which presents potential problems for women writers of the period:

> In the quest for the sublime women writers were curiously recalcitrant. By and large they withdrew from a vision which seemed to reach, without mediation to divinity. The grand marriages of sense and spirit....are typically absent in female writing. Rather, there is a crossing back, at the brink of visionary revelation, to the realms of ordinary, bodily experience....When women do write of sublimity, there is frequently apprehension, a tightening of tone as if permission were sought from a patriarchal power.[22]

Radcliffe, however, draws on the language and emotional experience of the sublime more powerfully and effectively than many other woman writers of the period, staking a claim to sublime discourse through her female characters' intense responsiveness to the emotional effects of sublime landscapes, but also subtly responding to its gendered implications by utilising the concept to explore ideas of male power and oppression. Anne K. Mellor has suggested that Radcliffe in fact rewrites the sublime from a female perspective in her novels, constructing 'an alternative, more positive representation of the sublime' as experienced through nature; while for Burke the experience is always predicated on fear, Mellor argues that 'Radcliffe anticipates Coleridge and Wordsworth in suggesting that one can reach this consciousness of the power and glory of divine creation without fear and trembling' (pp. 94-5), and within her novels the heroines frequently derive mental support and emotional strength from their contemplation of sublime landscapes. Mellor goes on to suggest that Radcliffe presents us with a second version of the sublime in which she displaces 'the horror of the Burkean sublime from nature into the home', so that 'sublime horror originates not from nature' as in Burke but 'rather from man' (p. 94 and p. 93).

Such critical readings suggest that, while appropriating Burkean terminology and concepts, Radcliffe's novels offer a complex negotiation with the ideas underpinning Burke's theories. The processes outlined by Mellor occur repeatedly in much of Radcliffe's fiction, where the language of the sublime is used to describe architectural symbols of patriarchal power and where the heroines' experience of a divine power generated by natural scenery has the effect of diminishing fears caused by the patriarchal authority which threatens them within the social sphere. Here and in relation to other key concepts of the period Radcliffe displays a tendency to interrogate and rework existing ideas in ways that begin to offer new perspectives on natural landscapes and how we relate to them. While clearly fascinated by the ideas on landscape emerging from aesthetic and philosophical contexts, it is perhaps her own intense personal responsiveness to natural scenery which pushes her to explore these ways of thinking and take them in new directions.

That Radcliffe attempted to move away from the formulaic quality of earlier landscape-writing was noted early on by John Ruskin. In his account of the move away from the artificial landscape art of Claude, Poussin, and Rosa – art which was 'falsely painted throughout, and presenting a deceptive appearance of truth to nature' – he cites Radcliffe as one of the first writers in which a distinct shift of attitude could be perceived:

the approach of a new era was marked by the appearance, and the enthusiastic reception, of writers who took true delight in those wild scenes of nature which had so long been despised.

I think the first two writers in whom the symptoms of a change are strongly manifested are Mrs. Radcliffe and Rousseau; in both of whom the love of scenery, though mingled in the one case with what was merely dramatic, and in the other with much that was pitifully morbid or vicious, was still itself genuine and intense, differing altogether in character from any sentiments previously traceable in literature. And then rapidly followed a group of writers, who expressed, in various ways, the more powerful or more pure feeling which had now become one of the strongest instincts of the age.[23]

Though Radcliffe has subsequently been categorised as a writer whose handling of landscape aligns closely with picturesque trends, for Ruskin she represents a moment of change, a primary rupturing of the artificial picturesque approach. Ruskin perceives that Radcliffe, in negotiating with these aesthetic discourses in her fiction, becomes one of the first writers to invest in a more 'genuine and intense' way with the landscape, and he suggests that the extreme popularity of her work indicates a commensurate enthusiasm in the reading public for a kind of landscape writing which moved beyond the older formulaic models. Some recognition of her role in bringing about the shift in responses to nature which we would define as characteristic of Romanticism has also been acknowledged in more critical accounts; as Dorothy McMillan argues for example, the 'uses to which Radcliffe puts her pictures, are, of course, less derivative than the aesthetic that sanctions them and in some ways prefigure the concerns of the male Romantic poets'.[24] Such claims though are prefigured by Ruskin who identifies Radcliffe as a writer who begins to take the literary response to landscape in a new direction, one which would ultimately lead to the development of a Wordsworthian poetics.

Observations *within the wider Continental tour*

WHILE RADCLIFFE'S FICTION provides one important context for the Lakes tour, the more immediate textual frame of the tour itself is equally critical. As previously noted, Radcliffe's published account of her visit to the Lakes was appended to one describing her travel experiences within Continental Europe. Jeanne Moskal argues that in this respect the full tour is 'rare, and perhaps unique, among Romantic-period travel books, in juxtaposing foreign with domestic travels', and as such Moskal reads *Journey* as a chronicle of 'national identity'.[25] This wider textual and geographical framework is certainly relevant to Radcliffe's reflections on the Lakes, since her response to this region is shaped by and juxtaposed with her earlier quite negative experiences of Continental Europe.

The first part of the Radcliffes' trip had commenced in late May 1794, just a few days after Radcliffe had received the first instalment of the very impressive royalties for *The Mysteries of Udolpho*.[26] Radcliffe and her husband sailed from Harwich to Helvoetsluys and spent some time sight-seeing in Holland before travelling into Germany. Ironically, her account of this part of their tour has generated a great deal of critical interest in relation to Romantic constructions of place; as Ingrid Kuczynski notes, no 'investigation into the development of the Romantic perception of the Rhine – the *Rheinromantik* – can afford to neglect Radcliffe'.[27] Here Radcliffe's experience is in many ways reminiscent of William and Dorothy Wordsworth's later unfavourable response to Germany, as documented in Dorothy's journal account of their 1798-1799 visit.[28] Like the Wordsworths, the Radcliffes found the country to be dirty with stagnant ill-smelling streets and uncomfortable accommodation. It was also badly affected by the ongoing conflict with France and, in both cases, the tourist experience is primarily that of disappointment. The ultimate goal of the Radcliffes though was not Germany itself but the Swiss Alps, a region which Radcliffe had described in her fiction but never seen. Arriving at the border of Switzerland Radcliffe caught her first glimpse of that 'country of all others in Europe the most astonishing and grand' (*Journey*, p. 273). However, on reaching the official border post, it was found that the Radcliffes' travel passes had been incorrectly marked to indicate that they were at this point returning to England. The Radcliffes' claims were put under investigation but the experience disturbed the travellers and rather than waiting to hear the outcome they decided to turn back. This turned out to have been a fortuitous decision since the area was under imminent threat of French invasion and some of the towns through which they had passed in July had fallen to the French shortly after their return to England. On the journey back to Holland they met frequently with evidence of conflict and, in the circumstances, it is unsurprising that their return to English soil engendered such a powerful sense of relief. They sailed back to England in late summer, having spent only around three months on the Continent. Radcliffe's relief at landing back on English shores is tangible in the language depicting the first glimpse of her homeland; 'the lighthouse on the South-Foreland' appears to her 'like a dawning star above the margin of the sea' and by contrast, looking back she perceives 'a long tract of the coast of France, like a dark streak of vapour' (*Journal*, p. 367). The release of the tensions they must have felt in the last few disturbing weeks is also apparent in the pleasure she describes at once more being on English soil:

> And we landed in England under impressions of delight more varied and strong than can be conceived, without referring to the joy of an escape from districts where there was scarcely an home for the natives, and to the love of our own country, greatly enhanced by all that had been seen of others (*Journey*, p. 370).

As a result of a fairly disastrous experience in Continental Europe, Radcliffe is clearly programmed to read what she sees in England in a positive light and is immediately 'struck by the superior appearance and manners of the people to those of the countries we had been lately accustomed to' (*ibid.*).

Having been deeply disappointed in their Continental tour and having failed to make it to the Alps, the Radcliffes made alternative plans for a northern English tour. This was a logical decision, since popular accounts of the Lakes had presented the region as a handy and more easily accessible alternative to the Alps.[29] Although the text itself indicates no break in the journey and implies that the Radcliffes travelled north immediately, they in fact spent the last few weeks of the summer in London, before embarking on the northern expedition towards the end of September. During this interval, Radcliffe had an unaccustomed brush with celebrity, attending a literary dinner which had been organised by her publisher to celebrate the return home of the 'Mistress of Udolpho' (see Norton, p. 115). Radcliffe's subsequent decision to set off for one of the most remote areas of England can perhaps be seen as not only a reaction to her experiences on the Continent, but also as a rejection of such public displays. Indeed, it is notable that what she celebrates and esteems most highly in her Lakeland travels is not simply the sublime scenery but also the fact that the area functions as a kind of retreat from political and other corrupting influences. Having left the empty pleasures of London behind, the Radcliffes journeyed northwards through Derbyshire and the Peak district, then up through Cheshire, Stockport, and Manchester before arriving at Lancaster. The latter is figured in *Journey* as the real imaginative starting point for the Lakes part of the tour, since from this vantage point she looks out 'to the bay of sea beyond, and to the Cumberland and Lancashire mountains'. This first glimpse of the region offers her 'a vision of Alps' and it is here that her unfulfilled ambitions for the Continental tour would finally be realised.

Observations *and the rise of Lake District Tourism*

A LONG WITH the contexts already described, Radcliffe's tour also needs
to be situated within the context of Lake District tourist literature. By
the time Radcliffe came to the Lakes in 1794 the region had already been
inscribed firmly into the picturesque tourist tradition. There are some key
texts which Radcliffe either mentions by name during her tour or alludes to in
such a way as to indicate a clear line of influence. The first of these is Thomas
Gray's *Journal* of his visit to the region. Gray completed a tour of the Lakes
in 1769 but his account of his travels was not published until 1775. Both
Wordsworth and Radcliffe privilege Gray's *Journal* over and above the other
earlier published accounts of the region, since his was the perspective of a poet
rather than that of a guide-writer *per se*. Moreover, there is a sense in Gray's
text that, while influenced by picturesque ideals, he is nonetheless attempting
to find his own language in which to describe his experiences. Radcliffe
makes some specific references to the influence of Gray during the course of
her narrative, informing the reader – for example – that she chooses to stay
at Old Buchanan's Inn in Penrith on the basis of his recommendation and
commenting that the view of the Lune valley is 'distinguished by the notice of
Mr. Gray'.

Along with Gray, Radcliffe had clearly also read that other major
contribution to picturesque Lakes tourism, Gilpin's *Observations, Relative
Chiefly to Picturesque Beauty, on Several Parts of England; particularly the
Mountains, and Lakes of Cumberland, and Westmoreland* (1786). Though
she does not make any overt allusions to Gilpin's text, her choice of the
word 'Observations' within her own title may perhaps be an implicit
acknowledgement of influence. Gilpin's work had clearly informed some
landscape passages within Radcliffe's fiction, in which there are occasional
allusions to his descriptions; in *Udolpho* for example she slightly misquotes
Gilpin's description of Derwentwater as 'Beauty lying in the lap of Horrour!'
in her description of the landscape surrounding the Alps.[30] Like virtually all
other travellers at this period, Radcliffe no doubt also carried a copy of Thomas
West's deeply influential, *Guide to the Lakes* (first edition 1778) since, as Peter
Bicknell notes, for 'nearly half a century it was carried by almost every visitor
to the Lakes'.[31] West's *Guide* was indeed the ubiquitous travel guide for all
visitors to the Lakes in the last quarter of the eighteenth century, though as I
will go on to suggest, Radcliffe seems less reliant on West than other travellers
of the period. She does, however, frequently make reference to gentlemen's
residences and estates which are marked on West's map during the course

of her tour.   It seems likely that she carried a copy of either the 3rd (1784), 4th (1789) or 5th edition (1793) of West, since editions from 1784 onwards contained a basic map of the Lakes (reproduced above, before introduction).

While Radcliffe does not explicitly cite West's *Guide* at all during her narrative, his earlier publication, *Antiquities of Furness* (1774), is an acknowledged influence. *Antiquities* is though a very different kind of study, being less a picturesque approach to the landscape and natural scenery, and more of a historical guide to one particular area within the region.   In many ways *Antiquities* seems to have appealed to Radcliffe more than West's later *Guide*, since she cites from it on several occasions and is clearly reliant on West's historical data in constructing her own account of Furness Abbey. Other sources which provided historical data were also clearly important to her background research on the region.   She alludes at one point to another late eighteenth-century historical study of the region, Richard Burn's *The History and Antiquities of the Counties of Westmorland and Cumberland* (1777) and on several occasions she repeats details which feature in James Clarke's account of the abbeys and other important buildings, in his *A Survey of the Lakes of Cumberland, Westmorland and Lancashire* (1787) suggesting that she also used his study to enrich her understanding of the human history of the Lakes.   Clarke's text is interesting in containing quite detailed historical data alongside the more usual topographical and descriptive material, and this multi-faceted approach to the region clearly appealed to Radcliffe as she seems to have studied his account quite closely.   Given Clarke's critique of earlier picturesque guides, Radcliffe's reading of *Survey* may well have encouraged her to develop her own more personal response to the region.   Along with West, Burn, and Clarke, Radcliffe also clearly draws on other, older, historical accounts of Cumberland and Westmoreland, such as William Camden's *Britannia* (1586), and her research is further supplemented by details gleaned through conversations with shepherd boys, hired guides, and other locals encountered during her travels.

As the next section will suggest, Radcliffe is influenced by the earlier published accounts of the region in varying degrees and in different ways, but she certainly seems concerned to establish her own response to the Lakes as something apart from the standard picturesque approach.   Wordsworth too owned copies of Gilpin and several different editions of West, and he alludes in passing to Gilpin, Gray, and West during the course of his own *Guide to the Lakes* (1835) in which he was also clearly concerned to carve out a new kind of travel text.   Like Wordsworth, Radcliffe is influenced by these writers but seeks to establish her own voice and perspectives.   Indeed, Talfourd notes that though she 'always travelled with a considerable number of books' she 'generally wrote, while Mr. Radcliffe derived amusement from reading them' (p. 11). While Radcliffe's tour is informed by a range of sources and while details from these secondary sources are often incorporated in her narrative, the majority of the tour is given over to her own impressions on what she herself saw during her travels. At one point she makes her intentions in this regard explicit, commenting that her narrative sets out rather to 'describe what the author has seen, than to enumerate what has been discovered by the researches of others'. It seems clear that Radcliffe did not in fact intend her own contribution to Lakes literature to be a guide book as such, rather she intended it to be read as a series of reflections on what she had encountered during her visit. In this sense her use of the term 'Observations' seems carefully chosen since the text offers the reader 'Observations' in both senses of the word: a careful and diligent noticing of details within the surroundings and also a commentary and reflection on those details.

For Radcliffe's contemporaries, one of the most marked differences between her text and the Lakes literature which had gone before was that this was a tour undertaken by a woman. The picturesque tradition had been owned by male writers and establishes itself around the hierarchical and gendered categories of landscape art, aesthetics, and philosophy – discourses and cultural forms from which women were by and large excluded. Some anxiety about venturing into this territory is perhaps suggested by the fact that the full text of *Journey* opens with Radcliffe establishing that the narrative was in some sense a co-production – a result of Radcliffe's interaction with her husband and their shared experiences. She notes in the preface that it was written 'from their mutual observation'.[32] While this to some extent protects Radcliffe from charges of transgressive behaviour (especially as she attributes information relating to economics or politics to her husband), it also means that she writes throughout from the perspective of 'we' rather than from the solitary 'I' which dominates so much male-authored Romantic-era literature. Kuczynski describes this as a 'symbiotic "we"' (p. 243) and it reminds us that her journey is not the product of a solitary male exploration but a shared experience between husband and wife. Radcliffe's warm construction of her husband in her preface as 'her nearest relative and friend', and her presentation of the tour as a shared literary endeavour, has some parallels with the creative relationship existing between Dorothy and William Wordsworth; in both cases, the resulting text seems a product of shared discussions, experiences, and journeys through the landscape. This co-joined voice is original within Lakes literature at this point and moves us away from the overly prescriptive gaze of the picturesque male-authored tour guide.

At the very heart of Radcliffe's tour is a description of her ascent of Skiddaw and though by the 1790s ascents of Skiddaw by pony were becoming popular with tourists (as attested to by the cairn she finds on the summit) her prioritisation of this experience and her fascination in detailing the new perspectives on landscapes which it offers, also sets her account apart from that of her most important predecessors. This 'newness' is to do with the way in which Radcliffe actually responds to the experience but also relates to her focus on a different kind of landscape exploration to that which had been predominant in the picturesque guides. Gray had abandoned a plan to climb Skiddaw and seemed put off by the tendency of the locals to refer to it 'with a sort of terror and aversion' (*Gray's Journal*, p. 71). Indeed, he was later satirised by Clarke in his *Survey* as having pulled down the blinds of his chaise to avoid having to witness the horrors of Skiddaw, a fabricated claim which nonetheless passed into Lake District myth. West's *Guide* also does not involve any significant ascents; as Bicknell notes, he was 'almost exclusively concerned with the lakes and pays little attention to the mountains except as background to his picture' (p. 33). By contrast Radcliffe is fascinated by mountains and repeatedly reflects on the ideas and emotions which are generated by the contemplation of their grandeur and by the new perspectives they offer.

The Radcliffes in the Lakes

HAVING SPENT a few weeks in London following their experiences on the Continent, Radcliffe and her husband set out in September 1794 for the Lakes. They thus make their visit to the region during that period of the year when Wordsworth considered it to be at its finest and when 'the scenery is....more diversified, more splendid, and beautiful'.[33] Their chosen mode of travel does little, however, to suggest their determination to approach the landscape in new ways. Unlike the Wordsworths who – five years later, in the bleak December of 1799 – would notoriously make part of their journey from Sockburn to Grasmere on foot, the Radcliffes travelled to and undertook much of their exploration within the Lakes using the conventional mode of travel available to respectable middle-class tourists: a horse drawn carriage. Though they probably made the main part of the journey North in a more substantial covered vehicle such as a hired post-chaise, they certainly embarked on some local excursions in a smaller open vehicle, since Radcliffe describes arriving at the Inn at Threlkeld having been 'blown about, for some hours, in an open chaise'. The tour at times provides a fascinating insight into the practical experience of early tourist travel, including information about the nature of

A Journey made by Post-Chaise from a painting by J. Pollard

Vintage postcard of 'A Gentleman driving a Lady in a Phaeton' by George Stubbs, 1787

traffic on the road. Radcliffe mentions for example the dreariness of travelling through heavy rain on the way from 'Kirby to Kendal', with their progress severely impeded by 'long trains of coal carts' which they jostled amongst and then overtook. Though most of their tour was conducted in an open chaise, several excursions were made on foot when, for example, a particular route was impassable by carriages or, immediately on arrival in Keswick, when the Radcliffes – no doubt feeling cramped after a long journey – left their carriage and walked down to Crow Park to view the Lake. Some quite substantial walks involving moderate ascents are also specifically mentioned and though Radcliffe's text does not always provide full details of these walking interludes, others can be assumed by the very nature of the landscape being explored, and Radcliffe's later travel journals confirm that both she and her husband were confident and enthusiastic walkers. In addition to journeys on foot and by coach at least one excursion, the ascent of Skiddaw, was made by pony which was, at the time, the standard mode of ascent for tourists.[34]

For most of the time the Radcliffes travelled alone but they frequently engage in conversation with local people encountered on their walks and some expeditions, such as the ascent of Skiddaw and the crossing of the sands, were undertaken with the aid of a local guide. While there is a tendency to ridicule some of the terror experienced by early visitors and their reliance on hired guides, we should remember that the Lakes presented difficult and unfamiliar terrain, and a detailed and accurate map of the area was not yet available to tourists. The dangers of getting lost in this remote and little known landscape were only too real to early travellers.

Like other visitors of the period, the Radcliffes would pause at coaching or tourist inns along the way and on a couple of occasions specific details of these are given in the tour. According to the Talfourd biography, which was written with the co-operation of her husband and fellow traveller, Radcliffe would write up her day's experiences in these inns:

> Mrs Radcliffe almost invariably employed snatches of time at the inns where she rested, in committing to paper the impressions and events of the day, which she could afterwards review at leisure – a happy mode of prolonging those vivid pleasures of life, for which she had a fine relish (Talfourd, p. 11).

There is a Wordsworthian emphasis here on emotions 'recollected in tranquillity' and Talfourd comments on the importance of this process for Radcliffe; he suggests that such a habit 'tends to impart a unity to our intellectual being. It enables us to live over again the unbroken line of existence; to gather up

The likelihood of getting lost during a Lakes tour is represented by Thomas Rowlandson in his satirical series of illustrations depicting the fortunes of Dr. Syntax, 1812

the precious drops of happiness, that they be not lost' (pp. 10-11). Talfourd goes on to say that later these notes which record Radcliffe's more immediate 'impressions' were worked up into 'a regular form' for publication and it is probably at this point that those more quotidian concerns of the traveller – such as details regarding when the horse needed to rest or occasions on which William had to lead the horse over difficult terrain – which appear in her later posthumously published travel diaries, were edited out of the text.

Despite their conventional mode of travel, Radcliffe shows herself to be surprisingly independent of West's influence from the outset, and was clearly keen to establish her own experience of the Lakes. Crucially she does not follow the very definite tour route prescribed by West, nor the route taken by Gray or Gilpin, preferring instead to carve out to her own approach and itinerary.[35] West's tour was of course predicated on the idea of visiting a series of specific viewing stations which he had identified around the Lakes and here again Radcliffe does not conform to the prescribed experience of the picturesque tourist. She ignores most of West's stations altogether and makes only occasional passing references to others. She acknowledges for example the existence of a West station above the King's Arms in Patterdale, noting that 'Among the rocks, that rose over it, is a station, which has been more frequently selected than any other on the lake by the painter', but this passing comment clearly indicates that her own concerns and preferred vantage points are different. The choosing of her own route and her lack of interest in experiencing the landscape via West's stations is an indicator of Radcliffe's keenness to set up an experience of the Lakes in her own terms and in so doing, to open up the possibility of a more personal imaginative response. A desire to 'see' the landscape in new ways is also signalled by the fact that during the course of her Lakes tour she makes no reference to the use of a Claude glass, that staple piece of equipment for the eighteenth-century picturesque tourist. Instead Radcliffe is insistent on using her own eyes and her own creative faculties to see this landscape. Though Radcliffe's perspective is still shaped to some extent by the ideals and discourse of the picturesque, during the course of these travels her encounters with the landscape repeatedly break free from this aesthetic frame into new imaginative realms.

In terms of their itinerary, while Gray approaches the Lakes from the East, Gilpin from the North, and West via the sands, the Radcliffes' travel across country from the south, via Lancaster. They journey through Caton, Hornby, and Melling, then into Kirkby Lonsdale where Radcliffe pauses to admire Devil's Bridge, 'a venerable Gothic bridge over the Lune, rising in tall arches, like an antient aqueduct'. Leaving Kirkby Lonsdale by the Kendal road they pass through Endmoor and spend the night at an inn in Kendal. After a day spent inspecting the various historic sites in Kendal in more detail they depart via Shap, heading for Bampton and Haweswater. Here they pause to explore the environs of Mardale Common before returning to Bampton, from where they press on to Ullswater, past Lowther Hall and down to Pooley Bridge. At Ullswater Radcliffe has her first really intense experience of Lakeland scenery and the landscape here clearly fulfils her desires for the sublime scenery which she had been denied in the Alps – it offers 'severe grandeur and sublimity; all that may give ideas of vast power and astonishing majesty' which 'awakens the mind to expectation still more awful' and 'touching all the powers of imagination, inspires that "fine phrensy" descriptive of the poet's eye'. They linger around the Lake for some time, travelling west along the northern shore of Ullswater and taking in Gowbarrow Park and Lyulph's Tower before arriving at Patterdale, where they spend a stormy night in the King's Arms Inn. The following day they travel back along the shores of Ullswater taking in Dalemain and Arthur's Round table, and continue on to Brougham Castle. The ruins of Brougham clearly appealed to Radcliffe and she lingers here and describes them in great detail before returning to Emont Bridge and travelling on to Penrith. After exploring the town, the Radcliffes leave by the Graystock road and, passing the area of Roman encampments, head towards Keswick, pausing at Castlerigg stone circle. Radcliffe does not specify where they stayed in Keswick but they probably followed Gray in choosing the Queen's Head (now the Queen's Hotel) in the centre of the town, which was then the town's 'premier tourist hotel'.[36]

On arriving in Keswick the Radcliffes leave their carriage and walk down to Crow Park to look at Derwentwater, which Radcliffe suggests, 'looked insignificant' and 'scarcely interesting' after the 'simple majesty of Ullswater'. They make Keswick their base for the next few days and undertake a number of day-long excursions from the town.   Keswick had already become the 'first Lakeland tourist resort' or what Bicknell calls, the 'established Elysium of the North' (pp. 6-7), but Radcliffe's disappointment at Derwentwater again registers her inclination to look for her own version of the Lakes and not simply follow the accepted tourist response to 'Keswick's favoured pool'.[37] The morning after their arrival the Radcliffes engage a guide and horses 'accustomed to the labour' and escape the busy town to undertake the ascent of Skiddaw, a five hour journey which Radcliffe describes in detail and which forms the real imaginative centre of the tour.   On a 'gray autumnal morning' they set off again from Keswick along the western shore of Bassenthwaite to circumnavigate the lake, then on a subsequent and more promisingly sunny morning they journey along the eastern shore of Derwentwater, past Lodore Falls heading for Borrowdale, by this date another key feature of the Lake District tourist itinerary.

Having explored the environs of Keswick over a number of days, the Radcliffes finally leave the town and journey south over Dunmail Raise. They pass through Grasmere and Rydal *en route* to Ambleside and Radcliffe favours both with praise, noting that at Rydal 'wherever art appears, it is with graceful plainness and meek subjection to nature'.   It is in Ambleside, 'a black and very antient little town,' that the Radcliffes first encounter Windermere, whose 'boundaries shewed nothing of the sublimity and little of the romantic wildness, that charms, or elevates in the scenery of the other lakes'.   While Radcliffe makes little comment on the number of visitors to Keswick, she is critical of the effects of tourism on the area around Windermere, which, a couple of decades later, Keats would also find to be 'disfigured' by the 'miasma of London'.[38] They explore the shores of the lake and take a trip on the ferry but Radcliffe writes that 'on the whole, Windermere was to us the least impressive of all of the lakes'.   She make no mention of them pausing to spend the night here and instead they press on rapidly towards Esthwaite and Hawkshead, then onto Coniston, which is depicted as 'sweetly seated under shelter of the rocks'. Coniston Water (which Radcliffe refers to as Thurston-Lake) is described as 'one of the most charming we had seen'.[39] They travel down to Lowick Bridge and then onto Ulverston, a 'neat but ancient town', which they do not reach till nightfall.   The following day they journey from Ulverston to Furness Abbey, which is an important focus point for Radcliffe and, in some ways, the culmination of her tour. From the Abbey the Radcliffes return to Ulverston and cross Morecambe Bay sands to return to Lancaster. Radcliffe ends the tour with an important summative reflection which serves to reinforce the key elements we are to carry with us from her encounter with the Lakes, and which reminds the reader of her dual interest in the beauty of the external physical landscapes and the wider socio-political significance of the region: 'Thither we returned and concluded a tour, which had afforded infinite delight in the grandeur of its landscapes and a reconciling view of human nature in the simplicity, integrity, and friendly disposition of the inhabitants'.

Contemporary Responses

A T THE TIME of its publication, Radcliffe's venture into travel-writing was received with enthusiasm by the reading public; *Journey* went into three editions in 1795 and the section describing her ride over Skiddaw was incorporated into all subsequent editions of West's *Guide*. As Bicknell notes, the 'revised *Guide* became a vade-mecum for Lake District visitors, and remained so for half a century' (Bicknell, p. 7) and Radcliffe's Skiddaw ascent was thus rapidly absorbed into the canonical Lakes tour literature of the period. The fact that a passage from Radcliffe's text was incorporated into the main Lakes guide not only indicates the extent of its popularity and influence, but also suggests that the Skiddaw passage was the aspect of the tour that contemporary readers felt added something new and important to the established literature of the Lakes.

The freshness of Radcliffe's approach to Lake District landscapes throughout her tour is borne out by the response in contemporary critical reviews, which were, on the whole, very positive about the work and in particular about the vibrancy of her description of natural subjects. While many did read Radcliffe's tour in relation to the popular picturesque movement, some reviews clearly perceive Radcliffe's prose account of the Lakes as subtly different to what had gone before. The *Critical Review* suggests that the popularity of her fiction had excited a 'public wish that she might engage in a work where the same talent should be necessarily employed to delineate the grandeur, beauty, or sublimity of real scenery' and commends her new work in this field, suggesting that 'Elaborate accuracy, just discrimination, the most acute feeling, and....the happiest selection of words and significant epithets are hers'; the review registers the sense that Radcliffe is trying to produce a new kind of language and writing about the Lakes when it suggests that her language 'is in some respects peculiar and unfamiliar,' being 'partly the language of poetry and partly of painting' (*Critical Response*, p. 43). The review further draws attention to Radcliffe's remarkable success in capturing the personal emotions which have been generated by the landscape, noting that the 'grandeur of the thought is expressed without the least possible diminution' so that the 'enthusiasm of the author is in a great degree imparted to the reader' (*ibid.*). In other words Radcliffe manages to convey in her prose not merely physical description but also the emotional effects of particular scenes, a development which positions her work as a crucial link in the movement towards Romantic ways of thinking about landscape. The reviewer clearly struggles at times to adequately define and describe this new kind of writing but suggests that external features are 'here brought together, enriched with successive images and nervous expression, and contribute to raise in the mind the highest emotion of perfect grandeur or sublimity' (*ibid.*). The *Analytical Review*, picks up on the extent to which Radcliffe leaves behind both the formulaic language of the picturesque and the trappings of her Gothic fiction, noting that Radcliffe pays careful attention to style within the tour and avoids the 'artificial diction' found in her novels as well as the 'representation of pathetic scenes or wonderful events'; instead she chooses to describe 'in neat and easy language, whatever, in the course of her travels, appeared worth describing' (*Critical Response*, p. 42).

Despite Walter Scott's measured praise of some of the landscape passages within her fiction in his 1824 'Prefatory Memoir', elsewhere in the piece he compares her fictional landscapes unfavourably to those of fellow novelist, Charlotte Smith, as being 'far from equal in accuracy and truth' and suggests that 'there is, as it were, a haze over her landscapes' (p. xxx). Scott goes on, however, to compare a descriptive passage from one of her novels to a passage from *Observations*, commenting that the latter displays the 'precision' of which she was capable when 'actually engaged in copying nature' (xxxiii-xxxiv). Scott commends her tour in his memoir as 'very well written' and notes of her visit to the 'Lakes of Westmoreland' that it was 'highly calculated to awaken her fancy, as nature has in these wild but beautiful regions realized the descriptions in which this authoress loved to indulge' (vi).

Talfourd makes a similar distinction between Radcliffe's fictional and non-fictional handling of natural landscapes in his 1826 'Memoir'. He suggests that in her fiction she 'writes of places, which she has not visited; and, like a true lover, invests absent nature with imaginary loveliness' (p. 75), but that within the Lakes section of *Journey* and other unpublished travel journals we see:

> How singularly capable Mrs. Radcliffe was of painting the external world, in
> its naked grandeur, her published tour among the English Lakes, and perhaps

still more, the notes made on her journeys for her own amusement, abundantly prove. In the first, the boldness and simplicity of her strokes, conveying the clear images to the eye of the mind, with scarcely any incrustation of sentiment, or perplexing dazzle of fancy, distinguish her from almost all other descriptive tourists (p. 74).

Although to a modern reader Radcliffe does at times seem to overlay her descriptions with a great deal of imagination and 'fancy' it is worth noting that in the context in which she was writing, her prose account of the Lakes stood out as unusually stripped back and simple. The attention to real landscapes is combined with her interest in the imaginative potential of those spaces, and this clearly situates Radcliffe's travel writing as a key milestone on the journey from the picturesque tour guides to the Lake Poets.

It is unsurprising that Radcliffe should venture outside the confines of the Gothic novel and produce a piece of travel writing given the close connections between her fiction and eighteenth-century landscape tourism, but there is some evidence that the effects of this literary experiment on her development as a writer are quite significant, a point which will be explored more fully in the next section. By the 1790s though there was already something of a backlash against the fashion for penning a Lakes tour and this, as well as the explicit connection between Radcliffean Gothic and Lakes tourism which had been drawn attention to by the publication of *Observations*, had some negative consequences, including turning Radcliffe into an easy object of ridicule. In his satirical play, *The Lakers* (published in 1798 though never performed), the clergyman and dramatist, James Plumptre, creates the character of 'Veronica', a novelist and a Lakes tourist, who plans to set her next Gothic novel in the region and who appears to be modelled on Radcliffe. Plumptre's satirical portrait was clearly a response to Radcliffe's published tour, which along with West's *Guide* is the text to which Plumptre directs any readers not acquainted with either the Lakes or the Lakers in his Preface. Moreover, the drama plays with the public's expectations that a Lakes-based Gothic novel would follow the tour:

You must know, Sir Charles, I have always several works in hand at the same time; and, as I always introduce a great deal of description of scenery in my romances, I keep that in my eye while I am travelling, and write a romance at the same time with my tour....I think I shall lay the scene of my next upon Derwent-water, make St. Herbert to have murdered a pilgrim, who shall turn out to be his brother, and I shall call it 'The Horrors of the Hermitage.' I can introduce a mysterious monk of Borrowdale, and shall have fine opportunities of describing luxurious groves and bowery lanes[.][40]

The high comedic value of this Gothic novelist-come-Lakes-tourist is emphasised by Plumptre in the preface to his play in which he indicates that he wanted the comic actress, Isabella Mattocks, to take on the part, suggesting that in her hands, it would 'produce a very laughable effect' (p. viii). While Radcliffe does occasionally lapse into those rather irritating fashionable phrases of the period with which Veronica's speech is littered, describing the scenery for example as 'inexpressibly sublime', she does not simply conform to the model of picturesque traveller so easily ridiculed by Plumptre and her account is much more complex and interesting than his very two-dimensional satirical portrait would suggest.

ATTIC MISCELLANY.

M.ʳ MATTOCKS as M.ʳˢ WARREN
in the Road to Ruin.

Mrs Isabella Mattocks, whom Plumptre identified as his choice of actress to play the fictional Gothic novelist

It does though seem entirely likely that Radcliffe considered the idea of producing a Lakes-based romance before starting out on the tour but, if this is the case, she clearly decided to abandon such a project, as she set her next novel, *The Italian*, in Southern Italy. There are a number of possible factors which might explain this decision, one of which is the growing satire directed towards the Lakers and towards publications invoking the scenery of the Lakes. A second possible consideration is the fact that one of her fellow novelists, and in many ways her closest literary rival at this point – Charlotte Smith – had already staked a claim to the region in her 1789 Gothic-sentimental novel, *Ethelinde; or, the Recluse of the Lake*, with its fictional Grasmere Abbey. Ironically it is Smith's fictional landscapes which Scott would later praise over Radcliffe's in his 'Prefatory Memoir'. Given that by the mid-1790s Smith was also a very popular novelist, Radcliffe may have decided that to go into direct competition with her over a Lakes-based romance was unwise. There is perhaps though a third and possibly more interesting reason why Radcliffe does not pen a Lakes novel following her tour, which relates to her having actually experienced the Lakes landscape in person. Such first-hand experience of real landscapes may well have revealed to Radcliffe the limitations of her earlier imaginary constructions of natural scenery and meant that this region was therefore problematised as a location for her fiction. That Radcliffe's experience of the Lakes landscape and her attempts to capture it in language had brought about a radical destabilisation of her own literary modes of representation, is a possibility which will be explored in the next section.

Re-reading Observations

WHILE RADCLIFFE'S LAKES tour has frequently been aligned with the picturesque tradition and subsequently dismissed from accounts of the development of literary responses to the region, her narrative is long overdue reconsideration. Closer analysis of *Observations* reveals that Radcliffe makes clear attempts to distinguish her approach and her commentary on the region from the picturesque guides which had gone before, and to find new ways of reading this landscape. This is in many ways an exploratory text which draws on a range of influences and discourses in order to offer a fresh literary and imaginative response to the landscape of the Lakes.

As a Gothic writer, attuned to the use of landscapes to convey heightened mood and feeling, Radcliffe clearly recognises the potential of a landscape which was still sending shudders through the spines of late eighteenth-century visitors. Reading the landscape in Gothic terms is one of her initial imaginative ways into the Lakes and – given her established reputation as the mistress of the genre – such an approach gives her a privileged imaginary access to a region whose meanings had been controlled and inscribed by male picturesque writers.

From the outset Radcliffe draws attention to the Gothic potential of this landscape and she signals this in the language and imagery of several early passages. She draws her readers in through this strategy and within the first few pages plays to what were no doubt the expectations of the reading public when turning to a travel guide by the 'mighty enchantress' herself. The 'clouds rolling' along the top of the Lune valley are 'like smoke from a cauldron' and here the 'venerable Gothic bridge over the Lune' rises 'in tall arches.' Kendal is the first major town encountered by the Radcliffes after Lancaster and it is presented initially as one of her fictional Gothic locations:

> white-smoking in the dark vale....the outlines of its ruinous castle were just
> distinguishable through the gloom, scattered in masses over the top of a small

round hill on the right. At the entrance to the town the river Kent dashed in
foam down a weir; beyond it, on a green slope, the gothic tower of the church
was half hid by a cluster of dark trees; gray fells glimmered in the distance.

A Gothic reading of the landscape recurs many times throughout *Observations*
as the Radcliffes progress through the region. Radcliffe repeatedly turns to the
language of witches, fantasy, and magic, frequently calling up that mood and
atmosphere of mystery which is ubiquitous in her fiction through allusions to
the world of fantasy and the supernatural: a lake is concealed within a 'rocky
cauldron'; we encounter 'wizard' glens and 'magical effect[s]'; 'tremendous
crags' resemble 'one of those beautifully fantastic scenes, which fable calls
up before the wand of the magician'. Though Radcliffe does move beyond
this discursive frame during the course of the tour, her Gothic treatment of
the region itself begins to open up new imaginative ways of perceiving the
landscape and challenges the prescriptive demands of the picturesque. Radcliffe
herself clearly recognised that this Gothic perspective was unusual within the
established canon of late eighteenth-century Lakeland tourist literature and
looks to the authority of older literary material in validating such impressions
of the landscape. In turning to more overtly literary sources Radcliffe shifts
away from the authority of landscape art-aesthetics, and this too provides her
with an alternative set of reference points with which to explore the imaginative
potential of the place. She describes the approach to Keswick, by this time the
main focus of popular tourist attention, as 'the very region, which the wild
fancy of a poet, like Shakespeare, would people with witches, and shew them at
their incantations, calling spirits from the clouds and spectres from the earth';
she goes on to suggest that the 'wildness, seclusion, and magical beauty of this
[Keswick] vale, seem indeed to render it the very abode for Milton's Comus,
'deep skilled in all his mother's witcheries'.

 Though Radcliffe is calling on the authority of a male literary tradition
here, her literary references seem carefully chosen and often function to
identify empowered female figures within the landscape. It is notable for
example that she depicts Shakespeare's witches as having the power to control
and manipulate the landscape and Radcliffe's choice of citation from Milton's
Comus is also suggestive. Radcliffe returns to this poem repeatedly in her
fiction but, as Angela Jones observes, it is significant that here she selects a line
from later in the poem which emphasises Comus's mother as being the 'source
of his powers', rather than the introductory line in which the son 'usurps the
mother' by 'excel[ling] her at her mighty art'.[41] Radcliffe's selective use of
male literary authority has here the effect of subtly connecting her own role as

enchantress with other empowered female literary characters.

While the importing of travel and landscape aesthetics into the Gothic novel discussed earlier was a widely recognised ingredient of her fiction, in *Observations* we have a reversal of the process, in which Radcliffe imports aspects of the language and expectations of Gothic romance into a travel guide. It is a fascinating experiment and one that further reveals the complexity of the relationship between these eighteenth-century modes of writing as well as Radcliffe's willingness to experiment with existing textual formulas. One consequence of her overlaying aspects of the Gothic formula on her travel text is that it predisposes her readers to perceive Radcliffe the traveller as her own autobiographically constructed heroine, who, like those fictional heroines, is emotionally responsive to the landscape through which she is travelling. As in her fiction, the reader is positioned to see what the female traveller sees and to feel what she feels.

One further side effect of the allusion to Milton's *Comus* is to overlay the experience of female travel with the same secret, partly sexual, thrill inherent in the experience of reading a Gothic novel, since within that poem the male sorcerer waylays a female traveller with his spells. Such an allusion in a text written by a woman journeying within this mysterious and potentially dangerous landscape has the effect of suggesting a shared experience of danger and excitement for the female tourist. The same kind of thrilling, because imagined, terror has long been recognised as an important factor in the popularity of the Gothic novel which were greedily received by an audience of bored middle-class women readers. Scott clearly recognised this source of Radcliffe's appeal, suggesting that: of her ability to maintain 'the thrilling attraction of awakened curiosity and suspended interest....every reader felt the force, from the sage in his study, to the group which assembles round the evening taper, to seek a solace from the toils of ordinary life by an excursion into the regions of imagination' (p. vi). It is this same potential for permitted and 'thrilling' excitement which is satirised by James Gillray in his 1802 Cartoon 'Tales of Wonder!' (see p. 34). The lines from *Comus* connect the experiences of the female tourist wandering in terrifying and mysterious landscapes with those of the heroines of Radcliffe's fictions. In overlaying the emotions of her Gothic heroines on the female traveller, she begins to take Lakes literature in new directions since she prioritises both female perspectives and a kind of very intense personal responsiveness. Radcliffe writes sensitively in *Observations* of how the changing landscape creates 'new shades of effect on the mind' and, as Robert Miles suggests, 'her ability to play upon the feeling mind unlocked more meanings than those fashionably encoded within the

'Tales of Wonder!' by James Gillray, 1802

sublime and picturesque' (p. 54). It is to a large extent this capacity to 'unlock' new meanings to those previously attached to this landscape which makes Radcliffe's tour so significant in terms of the evolution of Lakes literature.

Another consequence of the Gothic influence on Radcliffe's reading of the lakes is a fascination with the medieval past and the ancient history of the people in this region. In this too, Radcliffe's tour begins to deviate from the remit of the picturesque guide since she is almost as much interested in the traces of human history within the region as with the natural landscape itself. Radcliffe's interest in these relics goes far beyond fashionable interest in the aesthetic potential of ruined buildings since Radcliffe reads the landscape as a living historical document, bearing the traces of a trajectory of human history which moves from an older pagan past of Druid sacrifice, through a medieval period of Feudal power, and on into the revolutionary present. Hers is a lived-in and living landscape filled with imaginary voices from the past and incorporating 'peasants....singing merrily as they gathered the oats into sheafs' in the present. Despite its remoteness, Radcliffe depicts this as a landscape bearing graphic traces of its human inhabitants and in *Observations* we get a vivid sense of this as an inhabited landscape rather than one valued primarily for its aesthetic potential.

Unsurprisingly, Radcliffe repeatedly turns to Gothic locations and buildings, especially abbeys and castles, during the course of her journey and through these relics finds herself drawn back into the region's past. Her Gothic imagination allows her to take this one step further, however, and she often presents us with landscapes imaginatively re-inhabited by those long dead; near Bampton she finds 'sequestered and gloomily overshadowed' glades in which 'monks have glided beneath the solemn trees in garments scarcely distinguishable from the shades themselves' and, at Furness Abbey, such supernatural presences are powerfully felt:

> As....we rested opposite to the eastern window of the choir....the images and the manners of times, that were past, rose to recollection. The midnight procession of monks, clothed in white and bearing lighted tapers, appeared to the 'mind's eye'....when, at the moment of their entering the church, the deep chanting of voices was heard, and the organ swelled a solemn peal. To fancy, the strain still echoed feebly along the arcades and died in the breeze among the woods, the rustling leaves mingling with the close.

The meaning of these ancient Gothic architectural monuments takes on further significance during the course of Radcliffe's narrative in ways which also recall their function in her fiction. In particular she lingers over the way in which these symbols of feudal power have over time been reclaimed by nature; at Brougham castle a 'gloomy gateway, which had once sounded with the trumpets and horses of James the First', now serves 'only to shelter cattle from the storm' and the 'great hall' is 'now choked with rubbish and weeds'. She ends the passage with an image of nature's reclamation and of lingering human guilt for crimes against fellow man:

> Of the walls around us every ledge....were embossed with luxuriant vegetation. Tufts of the hawthorn seemed to grow from the solid stone, and slender saplings of ash waved over the deserted door-cases, where, at the transforming hour of twilight, the superstitious eye might mistake them for spectres of some earlier possessor of the castle, restless from guilt[.]

Furness Abbey, which appears at the end of the tour, is similarly reclaimed by nature in an image reminiscent of Shelley's depiction of the fallen fragments of the statue of an ancient king in his 1817 sonnet 'Ozymandias'; as in the poem, in which the statue lies in fragments and the sands have reclaimed the symbols of his power, so here 'the tower, that once crowned this building, having fallen, lies in vast fragments, now covered with earth and grass, and no longer distinguishable but by the hillock they form'.

This reclamation by nature of the old symbols of patriarchal feudal power is a trope deployed by other women writers during the 1790s and has deeply political implications, reminding the reader of the transience of all forms of social and economic power.[42] Radcliffe's literary career travels alongside one of the most significant political events in modern European history: the French Revolution and its aftermath, and this context shapes her fiction in a variety of ways. Her first novel was published in the same year in which the Bastille fell and her 'popularity was at its height as Revolutionary Terror swept France' (Norton, p. 11). As Robert Miles and other critics have shown, Radcliffe's writings respond to these events in a distanced way, but they do nonetheless respond to them. Her fiction is shaped by ideas which would inform the key debates of the period about the rights of the individual and powerlessness in the face of oppression and tyranny. Ongoing turbulence in France is the backdrop to Radcliffe's 1794 tour of the Lakes and we can sense her instinctive rejection of tyranny in this fascination with broken symbols of feudal power. In literature of the early 1790s images of ruined symbols of power function even more specifically as a reminder of Paris's infamous Bastille and all that it represented. Radcliffe's account of the ruins of Brougham Castle, for example, parallels contemporary published accounts of the Bastille, such as those by the poet Helen Maria Williams in her popular *Letters Written in France in the Summer of 1790*. On descending into the dungeons of the Bastille, Williams writes:

> We saw the hooks of those chains by which the prisoners were fastened by the neck to the walls of their cells – many of which, being below the level of the water, are in a constant state of humidity....Good God! – and to these regions of horror were human creatures dragged at the caprice of despotic power....There appear to be a greater number of these dungeons than one could have imagined the hard heart of tyranny itself would contrive, for, since the destruction of the building, many subterraneous cells have been discovered....Some skeletons were found in these recesses with irons still fastened on their decaying bones.[43]

Radcliffe's account of Brougham echoes this description in many respects, here she too reads and critiques similar signs of past tyranny in the building itself; the very thickness of the walls:

> exhibit symptoms of the cruelties, by which their first lords revenged upon others....Dungeons, secret passages and heavy iron rings remain to hint of unhappy wretches, who were, perhaps, rescued only by death from these

horrible engines of a tyrant's will. The bones probably of such victims are laid beneath the damp earth of these vaults.

This critique of tyranny and feudal power had a clear political meaning in 1794 and thus through her interest in the historical traces of the people of Cumbria, Radcliffe's text begins to formulate new politicised readings of this landscape. Should the reader be in any doubt of the political implications of her account, Radcliffe makes this point explicit within her description of Kendal:

> Kendal is built on the lower steeps of a hill that towers over the principal street, and bears on one of its brows a testimony to the independence of its inhabitants, an obelisk dedicated to liberty and to the memory of the Revolution in 1688. At a time when the memory of that revolution is reviled, and the praises of liberty itself endeavoured to be suppressed by the artifice of imputing to it the crimes of anarchy, it was impossible to omit any act of veneration to the blessings of this event. Being thus led to ascend the hill, we had a view of the country, over which it presides; a scene simple, great and free as the spirit revered amidst it.

Coming as it does at the outset of the journey this is a crucial passage, since it marks Kendal as the gateway to an ideal social region in which the inhabitants have achieved a freedom against certain forms of oppression and in which a spirit of liberty and independence has subsequently been developed. Given the date at which she was writing, this overt affirmation of liberty and her refusal to reject this ideal in the light of recent events in France is a surprisingly radical one. Miles suggests that *Observations* 'provides the most emphatic evidence of Radcliffe's own political opinions at a juncture when the public mood had shifted sharply against the optimism of 1791 and 1792' and had 'turned very sour indeed'; he observes that, given 'the political hysteria, Radcliffe's comments on the Kendal monument stand out as a brave defence of bourgeois freedoms', suggesting that 'Radcliffe's cool reaffirmation of Price's dissenting principles in 1795 may be taken as an index of deep political belief' (Miles, pp. 61-2 and pp. 63-4). Radcliffe goes on to remind the reader of this independence of spirit at various intervals within the text, pausing on the approach to Keswick for example to mention the 'true consciousness of independence, which labour and an ignorance of the vain appendages, falsely called luxuries, give to the inhabitants of these districts, is probably the cause of their superiority', a reading which foreshadows the ideology of place and statements about the value of rural living established by Wordsworth in his 1802 Preface to the *Lyrical Ballads* and other contemporary texts. For Radcliffe it is partly the remoteness and inaccessibility of the region, occasioned by the interruptions of 'inclosed waters and pathless mountains', which produces this unique character of the inhabitants, and their 'superior simplicity': 'Secluded from great towns and from examples of selfish splendour, their minds seem to act freely in the sphere of their own affairs, without interruption from envy and triumph, as to those of others'.

These are ideas which would subsequently be taken up by Wordsworth in his account of the shepherds and other dwellers of the vale of Grasmere, and would become defining features of his poetic reading of this region.[44] In terms of the development of Lakes literature Radcliffe's text is therefore crucial in its reading of the Lakes as not simply a place of important aesthetic value but as a haven of political contentment, a last retreat for the thinking man or woman from the political turbulence of Europe, where natural seclusion promotes an ideal life of simplicity, community, and peace and where one of the primary attributes of the mountains is their capacity to cocoon the region from corrupting external influence. It is this ideal which Wordsworth would take as his primary motif when he settled in the Lakes in 1799 and this same ideal which he comes to realise in his early Grasmere poetry. In 'Home at Grasmere' he repeatedly turns to the sense of being enclosed and protected by this place ('Embrace me , then ye hills, and close me in') as crucial to his desire to take one of its 'lowly dwellings for my home' (Wordsworth, *Major Works*, l. 129 and l. 53, p. 175 and p. 157). Like Radcliffe, Wordsworth perceives the region to be contained within itself and a retreat from these 'unhappy times' (l. 253, p. 180) – an idea which is encapsulated in one of the most powerful passages within the poem:

> Something that makes this individual Spot,
> This small abiding-place of many men,
> A termination, and a last retreat,
> A Centre, come from wheresoe'er you will,
> A Whole without dependence or defect,
> Made for itself and happy in itself,
> Perfect Contentment, Unity entire. (ll. 164-170, p. 178)

Radcliffe's thoughtful engagement with the human history of the region means that she is one of the first writers to draw upon contemporary ideas about the value of a life of rural seclusion in projecting an actual vision of such a life being lived in the Lakes.[45] Somewhat ironically, she focuses this idyllic vision on Mardale, a hamlet which would subsequently be overtaken in the most brutal way by the demands of developing urbanisation when it was submerged in 1935 as a result of the damming of Haweswater to create a reservoir to serve Manchester. In *Observations* Radcliffe depicts Mardale parsonage as a powerful emblem of domestic life in the region; it is a 'low, white building on a knoll, sheltered by the mountain and a grove of sycamores, with a small garden in front, falling towards the water'.[46] Within this 'enviable little residence' she describes a scene of domestic harmony enacted:

> Here, in the winter evening, a family circle, gathering round a blazing pile of wood on the hearth, might defy the weather and the world. It was delightful to picture such a party, happy in their home, in the sweet affections of kindred and in honest independence, conversing, working and reading occasionally, while the blast was struggling against the casement and the snow pelting on the roof.

The idealisation of a humble rural existence is a Rousseauvian trope but the specific image of rural domestic contentment draws also on Cowper's influential blank-verse poem of 1785, *The Task*. In book four, he depicts a winter evening in rural solitude: 'Now stir the fire, and close the shutters fast, / Let fall the curtains, wheel the sofa round' (ll. 35-6). Similar sources and ideas no doubt feed into Wordsworth's choice of his own a 'low, white building' in Grasmere, just four years after the publication of Radcliffe's text, and remind us again of the subtle parallels between two writers who are often perceived as being at a far remove from each other ideologically. By the time Radcliffe came to the Lakes Wordsworth and his sister had already begun to fantasise privately about a life of rural retirement in some simple cottage and indeed, just three months before Radcliffe herself arrived in the Lakes, they had their first brief taste of what such a life might entail when they moved into Windy Brow, a house overlooking the River Greta in Keswick, for a few weeks in the spring of 1794. Radcliffe's inclination to linger over this scene of rural domestic contentment in the Lake District, suggests that her own desire for a lifestyle removed from the pressures of town and commerce has much in common with the fantasy lifestyle being imagined by the two young Wordsworths at this point.[47] Had Wordsworth read Radcliffe's own account of this vision of domestic contentment between the time he spent at Windy Brow and his final realisation of this dream in a small cottage in Grasmere in December 1799, the passage would certainly have carried added symbolic significance for a man still struggling to deal with the pain and unhappiness engendered by his experiences in France, since Radcliffe reminds us forcibly of the contrast between this ideal rural life in the Lakes and the conflict in France. Seeing a book discussing these recent events at the Parsonage she notes: 'what scenes, to what display of human passions and human suffering did it open! How opposite to the simplicity, the innocence and the peace of these!'. As her earlier insistence on the liberty and independence of the people of the Lakes indicates, Radcliffe had begun to construct the region not only as a rural haven and a refuge from political conflict, but also as a place in which a very English kind of independence could be experienced, of the sort Wordsworth would later claim to have found here and which he would celebrate in his poetry. Radcliffe's text helps us to situate those 'Wordsworthian' tropes within the wider cultural development of such ideas during the last decade of the eighteenth-century, and to see his poetic construction of the region as one which builds on ideas developed within earlier Lake District writing.

While Radcliffe's tour repeatedly turns to human activity within the Lakes, she does of course also spend a great deal of time attempting to find a language with which to depict the natural landscape of the region and, in this too, Radcliffe reveals her impulse to move beyond the discourse and 'frame' of the picturesque. Radcliffe's rejection of the itinerary and stations of West, suggests a desire to find her own perspectives on this place but in other crucial ways her focus is very different. Though West indicates that the summits of some of the fells are accessible, the focus of his tour is of views from the ground or from less dramatic points of elevation. While West's primary interest lay in the lakes themselves, Radcliffe finds a more powerful source of appeal in the mountains which surround them. Though the final years of the eighteenth-century saw an increase in tourists including an ascent within their Lake District itinerary and while some accounts of these ascents had been published, the mainstream picturesque travel texts offer little engagement with this experience prior to Radcliffe.[48] Radcliffe's personal interest in mountains is of course partly a consequence of her ongoing fascination with the Burkean sublime and the emotional effects of certain landscapes on the human mind, and many of her descriptions of mountainous terrain do draw extensively on Burkean language. Such scenes also though encourage Radcliffe to explore the potential of the human imagination since the inability to fully visualise a mountain requires a further intervention of the creative mind; in her description of the fells around Ullswater she suggests that being allowed only 'partial glimpses of the gigantic shapes....leaves the imagination, thus elevated, to paint the "forms of things unseen"'. Radcliffe's fascination with mountains suggests a desire to move beyond a Burkean response in that, not satisfied with experiencing the sublime by gazing at the boundless immensity of mountains from below, she wishes to change her perspective and explore the still quite new experience of gazing outwards and downwards from the summit.

Skiddaw was for a long time wrongly regarded as England's highest mountain and by the 1790s was certainly fixed in the tourist consciousness. Radcliffe's account of an ascent of this fell therefore offers a timely intervention in the development of visitor experiences within the region and is, in many ways, the real heart of her tour. While critics have tended to focus on poking fun at Radcliffe's, fairly natural, alarm on making the ascent by pony while seated side-saddle they have, in so doing, ignored a powerful passage in which she describes the unusual perspective on the Lakes which is offered by her new vantage point. This is a key moment in which Radcliffe breaks down the frame of the picturesque model since, as Tim Fulford notes, the picturesque approach means that 'bodily and temporal experience in the landscape was elided, as was the landscape beyond the frame: its wider geographic, cultural, and historical elements were excluded'.[49] Within the Skiddaw passage Radcliffe's recording of her own anxieties and the physical effort experienced by the horses turns this instead into an embodied experience, and the frame of vision is fundamentally dismantled by the radical shifts in viewpoint and sight brought about through the climb. *En route* to the summit, as the horses begin to slow down and pant with the effort of making the ascent, Radcliffe registers the dizzying way in which perspectives and thus meanings were shifting before her gaze. Derwentwater 'dwindled on the eye to the smallness of a pond'. Her vision of the 'amphitheatre' of the lake's mountains means that fells are no longer seen as individual sublime spectacles or as a framing background for the lake, but as a collective panorama suggestive of the geological rupture out of which they emerged; this is 'a scenery to give ideas of the breaking up of the world'. The effort of the climb and the tendency for the turns in the ascent to block out distant views means that Radcliffe also suddenly pans down to the 'shades of turf and moss' over which the horses scrambled. Perspectives are radically destabilised from this height and angle, so that Saddleback, 'though really at a considerable distance, had, from the height of the two mountains, such an appearance of nearness, that it almost seemed as if we could spring to its side'. As she reaches the summit itself, the view is so difficult to deal with via the linguistic tools available to her, she feels that she can venture only to 'enumerate' rather than to describe. This is a crucial moment in which Radcliffe steps more firmly beyond picturesque modes and beyond her own Gothic inclinations to seek a new outlook on the Lakes which cannot be achieved from the prescribed stations, nor contained within an imaginary frame:

We stood on a pinnacle, commanding the whole dome of the sky. The prospects below, each of which had been before considered separately as a great scene, were now like miniature parts of the immense landscape.

The immensity of the scene offered to her gaze from a vantage point in excess of 3000 feet immediately challenges any picturesque inclination to contain small sections of a particular view in a manageable and structured way. She proceeds to attempt to find new ways of capturing such a visual experience in language, turning first to cartographical imagery in describing the Lakes spreading before her 'like a map', before going on to enumerate in precise detail, almost devoid of any superlatives or Gothic baggage, a detailed and precise account of this living 'map' as laid before her eyes.

Radcliffe's description of the view from the top of Skiddaw registers the still novel nature of this radically altered perspective on the Lakes landscape and in many ways foreshadows Wordsworth's subsequent and famous cloud perspective in his *Guide to the Lakes*. Like Radcliffe before him, Wordsworth attempts to break the limitations of the picture frame and to take in the Lakes as a unity:

I know not how to give the reader a distinct image of [the main outlines of the country]....than by requesting him to place himself with me, in imagination, upon some given point; let it be the top of either of the mountains, Great Gavel, or Scawfell; or, rather, let us suppose our station to be a cloud hanging midway between those two mountains, at not more than half a mile's distance from the summit of each, and not many yards above their highest elevation (*Guide to the Lakes,* pp. 41-2).

Though Wordsworth's passage has been credited with offering a radically new way of seeing and thinking about the region, Radcliffe's description from the summit of Skiddaw, which pre-dates Wordsworth's text by some 15 years, indicates her own willingness to move beyond the formulaic and prescribed ideas about the Lakes and suggests a similar desire to respond to the region in a different and more holistic way.

Despite such moments of rupture, Radcliffe does of course, at times, continue to draw on phrases and ideas drawn from the picturesque tradition. However, in *Observations* the language of art-aesthetics functions as only one strand of her exploratory piece of travel writing and, moreover, there is some evidence to show that Radcliffe not only experiments with alternative ideas and approaches but also begins to question the limitations of the discourse of the picturesque when faced with the real landscapes before her. As she approaches the pass of Borrowdale, a favoured location in earlier guides, she begins by drawing on the language of the earlier accounts and on her own Gothic resources:

> Dark rocks yawn at its entrance, terrific as the wildness of a maniac; and disclose a narrow pass, running up between mountains of granite, that are shook into almost every possible form of horror. All above resembles the accumulations of an earthquake; splintered, shivered, piled, amassed.

Within a few lines though, Radcliffe pauses with a sudden recognition of the inadequacy of these discursive modes and indeed at the impossibility of conveying such a spectacle in language, noting that 'description cannot paint.... the wildness of the mountains'. This experience recurs during the course of the tour as she experiences a growing awareness of her inability to capture the variety and nuances of real nature in the formulaic language of the sublime and the picturesque:

> It is difficult to spread varied pictures of such scenes before the imagination. A repetition of the same images of rock, wood and water, and the same epithets of grand, vast and sublime, which necessarily occur, must appear tautologous, on paper, though their archetypes in nature, ever varying In outline, or arrangement, exhibit new visions to the eye, and produce new shades of effect on the mind.

She feels herself torn by her 'wish to repeat the picture' of what she sees in language and 'a consciousness of the impossibility of doing so'. This sort of anxiety is not in evidence in Radcliffe's fictional landscape passages, in which she displays a much greater dependence on the discourse of the picturesque. As Dorothy McMillan argues, it appears to be the experience of visiting the actual landscapes, previously encountered only in art and travel writing, which generates Radcliffe's awareness of the limitations of her own previous linguistic modes in attempting to capture the essence of these natural landscapes in words:

> When Radcliffe came to make her actual journeys, she was, of course, unsurprisingly still powerfully influenced by the culturally constructed way of seeing and of describing that inform her fiction....But some uneasiness begins to show, and her account of her tour of the Lake District shows her increasingly aware of problems in the inexpressibility of the sublime and of the difficulties

attendant on the composition of prospects. The countryside will not always yield itself up to the habit of composition, the eye cannot retain that grip of the prospect that picturing demands (McMillan, p. 57).

One of the consequences of Radcliffe's growing sensitivity to the limitations of pre-existing modes of travel-discourse are moments in which she begins to produce a more experimental kind of writing, passages which prefigure both Radcliffe's own later travel journals and also the kind of place-writing we have come to connect with Dorothy Wordsworth. Perhaps the best example of Radcliffe's determination to move towards a simpler and more precise kind of prose in response to landscapes which appear at first indescribable, is in her account of the journey out of the Lakes across the sands of Morecambe Bay at the very end of the tour. Here Radcliffe is faced with another completely new kind of landscape, which seems to further challenge and resist expression within the standard travel discourses of the period. Only residual traces of the formulaic phrasing and proclamations of the picturesque guide are to be found in a passage which offers instead a nuanced and precise account of the sands crossing, and which allows for a personal experience of a living landscape to overcome the fixed expectations set up by the picturesque:

> We took the early part of the tide, and entered these vast and desolate plains before the sea had entirely left them, or the morning mists were sufficiently dissipated to allow a view of distant objects; but the grand sweep of the coast could be faintly traced, on the left, and a vast waste of sand stretching far below it, with mingled streaks of gray water, that heightened its dreary aspect. The tide was ebbing fast from our wheels, and its low murmur was interrupted, first, only by the shrill small cry of sea-gulls, unseen, whose hovering flight could be traced by the sound, near an island that began to dawn through the mist; and then, by the hoarser croaking of sea-geese, which took a wider range, for their shifting voices were heard from various quarters of the surrounding coast. The body of the sea, on the right, was still involved, and the distant mountains on our left, that crown the bay, were also viewless; but it was sublimely interesting to watch the heavy vapours beginning to move, then rolling in lengthening volumes over the scene, and, as they gradually dissipated, discovering through their veil the various objects they had concealed—fishermen with carts and nets stealing along the margin of the tide, little boats putting off from the shore, and, the view still enlarging as the vapours expanded, the main sea itself softening into the horizon, with here and there a dim sail moving in the hazy distance. The wide desolation of the sands, on the left, was animated only by some horsemen riding remotely in

groups towards Lancaster, along the winding edge of the water, and by a mussel-fisher in his cart trying to ford the channel we were approaching.

This is a deeply experiential passage in which sight and sound and movement are captured. We are presented not with a static artificial landscape but one which in fundamental ways cannot be fixed. It is ever in movement, ever shifting, so that the prose has to move with it, recording the subtle changes moment by moment. That Radcliffe captures the complex experience of crossing the sands so effectively here reveals the extent of her development as a topographical writer during the Lake District tour. The Cumbrian poet and topographical writer, Norman Nicholson, often quite hostile to the literary efforts of offcomers, includes Radcliffe's Morecambe Bay passage in his 1977 collection, *The Lake District: An Anthology,* and in *The Lakers* he acknowledges the effectiveness of Radcliffe's description in this passage, suggesting that she manages to capture the uniqueness of this landscape in surprising ways:

It was a journey through forbidden territory, a dash through no-man's-land, an expedition into a world that was not our world at all. Not even Wells's first men in the moon moved through a more strange, less human territory. Anne *[sic]* Radcliffe knew this very well. No one could evoke better than she could the tame terrors of her age – the shadow on the window, the silence in the ruined abbey. Yet when she came to the Lakes she left her ghosts behind her, turning instead to the tangible mystery of rock and tide. Her beautifully-written account of the return crossing, from Ulverston to Lancaster, reminds one of an eighteenth-century chalk drawing[.][50]

Though we should not downplay the importance of other elements of experimentalism in Radcliffe's reading of the Lakes, such as her use of Gothic ways of seeing, Radcliffe's sands passage demonstrates that she is willing to go beyond existing discursive models, even those for which she herself was best known, in attempting to find new ways of responding to and mapping this region in language. Radcliffe's willingness to experiment in her travel writing with such a range of ideas and styles, produces a complex text which moves us from the standard picturesque travel guides towards the significant developments in Lakes literature to come. As McMillan has suggested, it may well have been her real foray into the kind of sublime landscapes which she had only previously imagined, which forced Radcliffe to question her own fictional constructions: 'there is some evidence that the processes of travel, the observation of actual landscape and the effort to render it and its effects, worked towards a loss of conviction in the landscape strategies of the novels'; 'her experiences of real places is what may well have put an end to her fiction' (pp. 52 and p. 63). Alongside growing cultural anxieties about the Gothic, a key factor in Radcliffe's subsequent abandonment of the Gothic novel could then have been her real-life encounter with the sublime landscapes which had been at the heart of those texts. It is deeply ironic that a writer who had made natural landscapes such a central component of her novels, should have come to discover not only the limitations of contemporary approaches to describing such landscapes but also possibly, by extension, the limitations of her own fiction.

The Afterlife of Radcliffe's Lakes Tour

IT SEEMS APPROPRIATE to end with some commentary on the ghostly afterlife of Radcliffe's tour or at least some reflections on the ways in which a residual presence of her account of the Lakes may be traced in subsequent Lakes literature. The mapping of precise avenues of literary influence is always a problematic undertaking, not least because – as the previous section indicates – contemporaneous writers experience shared socio-cultural influences which may well result in parallel creative developments. Nonetheless, it is worth reminding ourselves that Radcliffe's published account of the Lakes pre-dates both the arrival of the so-called 'Lake Poets' in the region and also Wordsworth's most important attempts to construct a poetics of place. In recent years, there has been a growing critical awareness that Radcliffe played a more significant role in the development of ideas which we identify with Romanticism than has previously been acknowledged, with her most recent biographer claiming that 'Ann Radcliffe planted the seeds of the nature myth harvested by Wordsworth and Coleridge' (Norton, p. 251). To date though this line of influence has largely been mapped through the novels and the influence of Radcliffe's account of the Lakes landscape has remained unacknowledged by the Lake Poets and underplayed by critics. As the previous section suggests, however, Radcliffe's treatment of the region prefigures what would become identified as a Wordsworthian perspective on place in several crucial ways, but particularly in her idealisation of domestic rural living, in her identification of the region as a place of political independence, as well as in her attempts to move beyond picturesque modes.

While Radcliffe and Wordsworth subsequently came to be perceived as being at opposite poles of the cultural spectrum in the Romantic period, largely as a result of Wordsworth's critique of Radcliffe, it is worth remembering that there are a remarkable number of similarities in terms of their biographical and literary trajectories. Born just six years apart, both were attracted to poetry and landscape at an early age and were deeply influenced by the writings of Rousseau, in particular Rousseauvian ideas about the emotional and moral effects of man's engagement with natural landscapes. Both also shared a fascination with philosophical and aesthetic debates of the period regarding the effect of landscape on the mind of man. The foundation for their writing was a wide familiarity with the English poets and both would be influenced by older figures, especially Shakespeare and Milton, as well as by early pre-Romantic poets such as Thompson and Cowper. Both also had radical sympathies and a keen interest in ideas about liberty and human rights, as they developed in the late eighteenth-century. Though Wordsworth was notoriously dismissive of Radcliffe's fiction, their respective journeys as writers had followed very similar lines and their literary identities had been shaped by very similar reading and thinking. It is perhaps less surprising than we might at first assume that some of Radcliffe's ideas about the Lakes in *Observations* should be forerunners of those which Wordsworth would himself adopt in relation to this region.

Wordsworth's response to Radcliffe was, however, deeply negative and played a part in the rapid decline of her reputation in the nineteenth-century. By the time of his death, Wordsworth's cultural influence was significant, and his criticisms of female sentimental novelists did much to sway public opinion. These attacks began early; alongside the manifesto for his own poetics in the Preface to *Lyrical Ballads* was an attack on 'frantic novels' and other forms of writing that display a 'degrading thirst after outrageous stimulation', which would seem to be targeted particularly at the Radcliffean Gothic mode (Wordsworth, *Major Works,* p. 599). Certainly, in a later private attack on Scott, Wordsworth also wrote explicitly of 'that want of taste, which is universal among modern novels of the Radcliffe school'.[51] His apparent dismissal of everything Radcliffe represented makes it difficult to trace more nuanced patterns of reading and responsiveness. In *Wordsworth's Reading*, Wu notes that Wordsworth had certainly read *The Romance of the Forest* and *The Italian* and in relation to the latter he cites De Quincey's account of this: 'One of Mrs Radcliffe's romances, viz. "The Italian," he had by some strange accident, read, - read, but only to laugh at it'.[52] Wu in fact makes no mention of Wordsworth having read *Observations* but as he did in fact own a copy of the 6th edition of West, which contained Radcliffe's account of the ascent of Skiddaw, some familiarity with this part of her account can at least be assumed.[53] Indeed, Wordsworth's views on Radcliffe's fiction notwithstanding, it seems highly unlikely that he would not have read a contemporary account of the region by such a significant figure on the literary scene during a period when he had begun to reflect on his own imaginative relationship with the landscape of his childhood, and despite the absence of any commentary by Wordsworth on the text, some Wordsworthian scholars have assumed a familiarity with Radcliffe's tour.[54]

Samuel Taylor Coleridge too was critical of Radcliffean fiction and indeed had written a 'severe' review of *The Italian* in 1798 for the *Critical Review;* he later though admitted to having torn it up following some negative feedback from Dorothy Wordsworth and in the end a more favourable review was published by another critic.[55] Coleridge had been engaged in writing a batch of reviews on Gothic novels at the time for the *Critical Review* and he wrote scathingly to William Lisle Bowles of the formulaic nature of such fiction:

> I am almost weary of the Terrible, having been a hireling in the Critical Review
> for these last six or eight months – I have been lately reviewing the Monk, the
> Italian....&c. &c. & &c. – in all of which dungeons, and old castles & solitary
> Houses by the Sea Side, & Caverns, & Woods, & extraordinary characters, &
> all of the tribe of Horror & Mystery, have crowded on me – even to surfeiting.[56]

Though Coleridge apparently shared Wordsworth's dislike of the Gothic novel, from the late 1790s onwards his own work displayed a fascination with the Gothic mode and the supernatural in poetry, and it seems that contemporary readers were sensitive to Radcliffean overtones in his work. When his poem, 'The Mad Monk' first appeared in the *Morning Post* in 1800 it was published with the following subtitle: 'An Ode; in Mrs Ratcliff's *[sic]* manner', an addition presumably added by the editor. While there has also been some later critical acknowledgement of the ways in which Radcliffe's fiction influenced the development of Coleridge's poetry, no line of influence between her Lakes tour and Coleridge's own, subsequent, Gothic response to the Lakes has been suggested. Given that *Observations* was reviewed in the main journals of the period, including the *Critical Review* (in July 1795), it would seem likely that Coleridge too was familiar with *Observations,* a text which is lacking the overly formulaic elements which Coleridge found so easy to ridicule in Radcliffe's novels and which in fact contemporary reviewers identified as offering new perspectives on the Lakes. It is therefore perhaps worth remembering that when Coleridge settled in the Lake District in the summer of 1800, seeking to establish his own poetic response to this place, his first poems set out to explore

the landscape for its Gothic potential.[57] Coleridge's early Gothic use of the
Lakes scenery in book two of 'Christabel', the poem on which he was working
during his first few months in the Lakes, is at times reminiscent of Radcliffe's
imaginative handling of the region and Coleridge too reads the landscape
as suggestive of an atmosphere appropriate to 'daylight witchery' and the
supernatural.[58] In the opening of book two, the Lakes landscape functions to
suggest danger for the female heroine, Christabel, who wakes from her night-
time encounter with the sexualised supernatural figure Geraldine, to the sound
of bells being pulled by ghostly sextons and echoing across the Lakes:

> In Langdale Pike and Witch's Lair,
> And Dungeon-ghyll so foully rent,
> With ropes of rock and bells of air.[59]

Radcliffe's imaginative portrayal of haunting sounds from the past being
carried on the breeze and groans emerging from abandoned dungeons is also
subtly paralleled by Coleridge's treatment of the wind echoing the cries of
human misery in his final major Lakes poem, 'Dejection: an Ode', in which
Coleridge, struggling under his own emotional burdens, finds the landscape
and its darker suggestions too difficult to bear.[60] Though such ideas and images
could well have developed spontaneously for the two writers, had Coleridge
read Radcliffe's account of the Lakes prior to taking up residence there in
1800, it is certainly possible that some aspects of her Gothic response to the
landscape entered into his imagination and helped to provide an alternative
way of thinking about the place to that which was being established and
owned by Wordsworth.

Though the Gothic would remain a marginal strand in Wordsworth's
poetry, scholars have pointed to Radcliffe's unacknowledged influence on at
least one of his early Lake District texts in which he was beginning to find
his own voice in relation to place. *The Borderers,* Wordsworth's only play, was
written between 1796-7. Work on this text therefore commenced just one
year after *Observations* was published and at a time when Wordsworth was still
living away from the region. While critics have pointed to Radcliffe's fiction
(and especially *The Romance of the Forest)* rather than the tour as an influence
on his Gothic handling of the material in the text, *Observations* cannot be
discounted as having played a role in shaping Wordsworth's treatment of the
region here.[61]

In an essay on the 'Genesis of *The Borderers*', John Harrington Smith
points out that the 'country of *The Borderers* is the Wordsworth country, yet

it is here made to represent an aspect of wildness and terror not met with elsewhere in Wordsworth's work'.[62] Smith, however, puts forward a case to suggest that the key source of influence in shaping Wordsworth's Gothic handling of the Lakes in the play is Gilpin's *Observations*. While there seems little doubt that Wordsworth did indeed consult Gilpin when working on the text, such influence does not wholly account for the unusually Gothic elements in the play and there is some textual evidence to suggest that Wordsworth may also have had the handling of the landscape by the established mistress of the Gothic in his mind while working on his drama. Smith suggests that Wordsworth modelled his ruined castle on the ruins of Brougham Castle near Penrith, but tellingly, in his support for this and for the presence of dungeons at the site such as those featured in the play, he footnotes *not* Gilpin – who offers only a brief account of the ruin – but Radcliffe's *Observations*, without any acknowledgement that Wordsworth too may therefore have turned to Radcliffe's account of the castle and its dungeons in writing his play. Indeed it is the dungeons of the castle which play the most significant role in the pivotal scene within *The Borderers* and, given Radcliffe's own imaginative rendering of these dungeons in *Observations* along with her detailed and lengthy depiction of the Gothic atmosphere of the castle itself, it is worth considering the possibility that Radcliffe's account may have informed Wordsworth's handling of this Lake District location within the play. Radcliffe presents the dungeons to the reader in graphic terms as a site of death and misery, and even goes so far as to imagine the 'echo of that groan below'; since in Wordsworth's play, Ferdinand contemplates a murder in the dungeons, there would seem to be some grounds for identifying Radcliffe's treatment of Brougham Castle in *Observations* as an influence on his Gothic handling of this location. A further important connection is suggested by the fact that in her treatment of the ruins Radcliffe links this site explicitly to the border riots which form the immediate context for Wordsworth's text, describing it as 'once among the strongest and most important of the border fortresses'.

While neither Wordsworth nor Coleridge would acknowledge any Radcliffean influence on their own early experimental responses to the Lakes, it is possible to trace the contemporary impact of *Observations* both through the inclusion of the key Skiddaw passage in subsequent editions of West's *Guide* and through references made by other writers and poets of the period. Thomas De Quincey, who moved into Dove Cottage in 1809, after many years of being fascinated by the region from a distance, describes the source of the region's appeal in his extended 1856 *Confessions of an English Opium Eater*. Here De Quincey points to Radcliffe's account of the 'fairy little domain of the English Lakes', which brought the region into 'sunny splendour', as being one of the main influences on his early imaginative construction of the place; he famously describes Radcliffe in this passage as 'the great enchantress of that generation' and refers to Wordsworth's residence in the place as a *later* but deeper 'magnet'.[63] John Keats, just before setting out on his own momentous journey north in 1818, wrote to his friend John Reynolds to say that 'I am going among Scenery whence I intend to tip you the Damosel Radcliffe – I'll cavern you, and grotto you, and waterfall you, and wood you, and water you, and immense-rock you, and tremendous sound you, and solitude you' (*Selected Letters of John Keats,* p. 102). There is clearly a great deal of satire targeted at the Radcliffean style in these lines, which were written at a point at which Keats was a devotee of Wordsworth, nonetheless this comment reminds us just how well known Radcliffe's account of the Lakes was within Romantic contexts, since Keats is able here to satirise some of the tour's stylistic traits with just a few shorthand gestures.[64] Keats would go on to make his own ascent of Skiddaw, having previously written to his brother of the pleasures of an ascent in terms which also suggests a memory of Radcliffe's earlier account of the experience: 'I will clamber through the Clouds and exist' (*Selected Letters of John Keats*, p. 111). Such references clearly indicate that Radcliffe's response to the Lakes remained at the forefront of cultural accounts of the Lakes even within second generation Romantic contexts, at a time when the Gothic novel had fallen out of favour and after the publication of influential Wordsworthian poems of place such as *The Excursion.*

By the later years of the nineteenth-century, however, with the Wordsworthian perspective firmly embedded in the cultural narrative of the Lakes and with Wordsworth's own rejection of the Radcliffe school of writing entrenched in the public mind, both Radcliffe's fiction and her account of the Lakes came to be increasingly sidelined and dismissed. In the Preface to *The Lake Country* (1864) Eliza Lynn Linton rejects Radcliffe by identifying her as a key proponent of the – by this date – deeply unfashionable picturesque movement:

> It is long since any book was written descriptive of the Lake Country. Green, and West, and Mrs. Radcliffe, and others of the Picturesque School, gave their absurdly exaggerated accounts of what they saw and perilled in these 'inhospitable regions,' as it was then the fashion to call them[.][65]

Linton goes on to satirise the terror of these writers and suggests that such 'idealistic' perspectives on the region were no longer of interest to the Lakes visitor. By the time Canon Rawnsley came to write his account of the *Literary Associations of the English Lakes* in the closing years of the nineteenth-century, Radcliffe's account had been completely subsumed within a narrative structured around the great male poets and writers, and dominated by the perspectives offered by the 'Bard of Rydal'. Radcliffe is awarded only a passing mention in volume one and Rawnsley offers a reductive approach from the outset, terming her this 'good dame' and offering a condescending account of her description of the ascent of Skiddaw in which she is gently ridiculed along gendered lines:

> We may....join the gallant Mrs. Radcliffe who rode over Skiddaw in 1794, and left behind her such an account of the terrible danger and difficulty of making this, apparently, the first ascent, by womankind, of our tremendous mountain, as would lead one to believe that, at anyrate in her mind, the feat was equal to a climb up Chimborazo, Cotopaxi, Kilimangaro *[sic]*, or the Mountains of the Moon....It was in sooth only by special providence and the extreme care of her guide that Mrs. Radcliffe....ever returned from that awful wilderness, those tremendous wilds; ever, in short, reached the valley alive.[66]

The satirisation of Radcliffe stretching from the Lake Poets onwards is revealing and points perhaps to a peculiar kind of anxiety of influence. As one recent critic remarks, 'No English writer of such historic importance and diverse influence has been so often trivialised by her critics'.[67] While the influence of male literary fathers is problematic, that of literary mothers is even more so. Indeed, Keats's disparaging reference to her as 'mother Radcliff' *[sic]* and his other attempts to diminish her status have been seen by recent critics as a response to cultural anxieties about his own involvement with the feminised genre of romance (*Selected Letters of John Keats,* p. 257).[68] Norton argues that 'The Romantic poets seem to have had a hidden agenda to purloin Ann Radcliffe's material for masculine poetry....Many "serious" male poets borrowed the poetic phrases and techniques of her novels, while doing their best to cover the traces of their influence' (Norton, p. 250). Wordsworth's public attack on the Gothic novel and on the writers associated with it, no doubt did a great deal to fuel the subsequent neglect of Radcliffe and the silencing of a Radcliffean line of influence, which only began to be seriously challenged with new developments in Romanticism scholarship in the late twentieth-century. While lines of influence and re-visionary readings in relation to Radcliffe's fiction are now well-established, her travel writing is still in the process of critical recovery, and much work needs to be done on a writer who has been almost completely written out of accounts of early literary responses to the Lake District. The first step in recovering Radcliffe's place within our understanding of the development of literary responses to the Lake District is to re-familiarise ourselves with the prose account of her visit. This edition allows a new generation of readers to experience Radcliffe's often experimental approach to writing the region, in a text which shows how early writers negotiated with a landscape that was still in the process of imaginative discovery, and which explores ideas about the Lakes which would subsequently, through Wordsworth's poetry and prose, become ubiquitous.

Notes to Introduction

1   Radcliffe's account of her tour of the Lakes was appended to a longer narrative detailing her experiences of visiting the Continent in the summer of that year. The title of the full tour as published was *A Journey Made in the Summer of 1794, through Holland and the Western Frontier of Germany, With a Return Down the Rhine: To Which are Added Observations during a Tour to the Lakes of Lancashire, Westmoreland, and Cumberland* (London: G. G. and J. Robinson, 1795). Hereafter the Lakes section of the tour will be referred to as *Observations* and the full text will be referred to as *Journey* with page numbers to the 1795 edition given in parenthesis.

2   Other important female Romantic-era writers who contribute to the development of literary responses to the region include the poet, Amelia Opie, who came to the Lakes in the 1790s and wrote poetry inspired by her visit – including an 'Ode to Borrowdale in Cumberland' (written in 1794 but published in 1808), and 'Allen Brooke of Windermere' (published in 1796) – and the popular sentimental novelist of the period, Charlotte Smith, who produced the first fictional treatment of Grasmere in her novel of 1789, *Ethelinde; or, The Recluse of the Lake*.

3   Rictor Norton, *Mistress of Udolpho: The Life of Ann Radcliffe* (London and New York: Leicester University Press, 1999), p. x.

4   Thomas Noon Talfourd, 'Memoir of the Life and Writings of Mrs Radcliffe', prefixed to *Gaston de Blondeville, or The Court of Henry III. Keeping Festival in Ardanne, A Romance,* by Ann Radcliffe (Philadelphia: Carey and Lea, 1826), pp. 3-83 (p. 3).

5   Sir Walter Scott, 'Prefatory Memoir to Mrs Ann Radcliffe', prefixed to *The Novels of Mrs Ann Radcliffe*, Ballantyne's Novelist's Library (London: Hurst, Robinson; Edinburgh: James Ballantyne, 1824), pp. i-xxxix (p. vii & pp. xvii-xviii).

6   Norton speculates that the absence of letters and private papers may relate to events at the end of her husband's life. Less than three years after his wife's death William Radcliffe married his housekeeper and shortly afterwards moved to France, dying in Versailles. See Norton p. 249.

7 'Mrs Ann Radcliffe', *The Annual Biography and Obituary, for the Year 1824*, 8 (1824), pp. 89-105. Hereafter referred to as 'Mrs Ann Radcliffe' with page numbers given in parenthesis.

8 Cited in Norton, p. 248. Both the 1824 obituary and the Talfourd 'Memoir' provide basic biographical information which was not significantly added to until the publication of Norton's full-scale 1999 biography. Norton's rigorous research has revealed many important new details about Radcliffe's life but does not radically question the basic biographical information about her early years which was made available at the time of her death.

9 Bonamy Dobrée, 'Introduction', *The Mysteries of Udolpho* by Ann Radcliffe (Oxford: Oxford University Press, 1980), pp. v-xiv (p. v).

10 Nathan Drake cited in Norton, p. 128.

11 Cited in Maggie Kilgour, *The Rise of the Gothic Novel* (Abingdon and New York: Routledge, 1997), p. 113.

12 Cited in Norton, p. 1.

13 *The Critical Response to Ann Radcliffe*, ed. Deborah D. Rogers (Westport, Connecticut: 1994), p. 44. Hereafter referred to as *Critical Response* with page numbers given in parenthesis.

14 Edmund Burke, *A Philosophical Enquiry into the Origin of our Ideas of the Sublime and Beautiful*, ed. Adam Phillips (Oxford: Oxford University Press, 1990), p. 53.

15 Ann Radcliffe, *The Romance of the Forest* (Oxford: Oxford University Press, 1986), p. 273; Ann Radcliffe, *The Italian* (Oxford: Oxford University Press, 1986), p.63.

16 A Claude glass was an indispensible piece of equipment for the eighteenth-century picturesque traveller. It was a small, slightly concave, tinted mirror which could be carried in the pocket. The tourist would turn their back on the actual landscape and contemplate it instead as reflected in the mirror, thus containing a section of that landscape within a frame and further imposing a painterly quality by the removal of some detail and sharpness. The major picturesque writers: Thomas Gray, Thomas West, and William Gilpin, all advocate use of the Claude glass.

17 Ann Radcliffe, *The Mysteries of Udolpho* (Oxford: Oxford University Press, 1980), p. 30.

18 *The Romance of the Forest* has been described as 'a Rousseauistic *Bildungsroman*' (Norton, p. 84) and Chard notes that it 'incorporates a large number of references to Rousseau's *Emile* (1762)....in its account of La Luc, the benevolent Savoyard clergyman who takes Adeline into his family'. Chloe Chard, 'Introduction', *The Romance of the Forest* by Ann Radcliffe (Oxford: Oxford University Press, 1986, pp. vii-xxiv (p. xxiii).

19 Ann Radcliffe, *The Castles of Athlin and Dunbayne*, ed. Alison Milbank (Oxford: Oxford University Press, 1995), p. 5.

20 Milbank notes that 'Charlotte Smith, Radcliffe's respected contemporary, also included poetry in her novels, but it is in Radcliffe particularly that verse is important both as expressive of individual feeling and as part of a claim for high literary status for the novel. Rather more of her poems are put in the mouths of female characters'. 'Explanatory Notes', *A Sicilian Romance* by Ann Radcliffe (Oxford: Oxford University Press, 1993), p. 204.

21 Robert Miles, *Ann Radcliffe: the Great Enchantress* (Manchester: Manchester

University Press, 1995), p. 32.

22 Anne K. Mellor, *Romanticism and Gender* (London: Routledge, 1993), p. 85 and Meena Alexander, *Women in Romanticism* (Houndmills: Macmillan, 1989), p. 167.

23 John Ruskin, 'Turner and his Works', *The Works of John Ruskin*, ed. E. T. Cook and Alexander Weddeburn, 12 vols (London: George Allen, 1904), XII, p. 117 and p. 120.

24 Dorothy McMillan, 'The Secret of Ann Radcliffe's English Travels', in *Romantic Geographies: Discourses of Travel 1775-1844* ed. Amanda Gilroy (Manchester: Manchester UP, 2000), pp. 51-67 (p. 55). DeLucia and Bohls have also put forward critical arguments to suggest that Radcliffe begins to destabilise the aesthetic framework of the picturesque. See Elizabeth A. Bohls, *Women Travel Writers and the Language of Aesthetics, 1716-1818* (Cambridge: Cambridge University Press, 1995) and JoEllen DeLucia, 'Transnational Aesthetics in Ann Radcliffe's *A Journey Made in the Summer of 1794 [...]* (1795)', in *Ann Radcliffe, Romanticism and the Gothic,* ed. Dale Townshend and Angela Wright (Cambridge: Cambridge University Press, 2014), pp. 135-150.

25 Jeanne Moskal, 'Ann Radcliffe's Lake District', *The Wordsworth Circle* 31: 1 (Winter 2000), 56-62 (p. 57 and p. 56). Both Moskal and DeLucia (2014) offer more detailed, though very different, readings of the way in which *Journey* juxtaposes Radcliffe's foreign and English travels.

26 Radcliffe received £500 in royalties for *Udolpho*, a sum so large that when the well-known and experienced publisher, Thomas Cadell, was informed that such an amount had been paid, he offered a £10 wager that it was not true ('Mrs Ann Radcliffe', p. 96).

27 Ingrid Kuczynski, 'Reading a Landscape: Ann Radcliffe's *A Journey Made in the Summer of 1794, Through Holland and the Western Frontier of Germany, With a Return Down the Rhine'*, in *British Romantics as Readers: Intertextualities, Maps of Misreading, Reinterpretations,* ed. Michael Gassenmeier *et al* (Heidelberg: Universitätsverlag C. Winter, 1998), pp. 241-257 (p. 242).

28 For a detailed discussion of Dorothy Wordsworth's journal account of her visit to Germany see chapter 4 of Lucy Newlyn, *William and Dorothy Wordsworth: All in Each Other* (Oxford: Oxford University Press, 2013).

29 Thomas West notes that: 'those who intend to make the continental tour should begin here; as it will give, in miniature, an idea of what they are to meet with there, in traversing the *Alps*'. *A Guide to the Lakes,* 4th edn. (London: Richardson *et al,* 1789), p. 5. Hereafter abbreviated to West, *Guide* with page numbers given in parenthesis.

30 Radcliffe refers to the Alpine landscape as 'beauty sleeping in the lap of horror' (*The Mysteries of Udolpho,* p. 55).

31 Peter Bicknell, *The Picturesque Scenery of the Lake District* (Winchester: St Paul's Bibliographies, 1990), p. 33.

32 *Journey* opens with the following address 'To the Reader' (p. v):
    THE Author begs leave to observe, in explanation of the use made of the plural term in the following pages, that, her journey having been performed in the company of her nearest relative and friend, the account of it has been written so much from

their mutual observation, that there would be a deception in permitting the book to appear, without some acknowledgment, which may distinguish it from works entirely her own. The title page would, therefore, have contained the joint names of her husband and herself, if this mode of appearing before the Public, besides being thought by that relative a greater acknowledgement than was due to his share of the work, had not seemed liable to the imputation of a design to attract attention by extraordinary novelty. It is, however, necessary to her own satisfaction, that some notice should be taken of this assistance. She may therefore, be permitted to intrude a few more words, as to this subject, by saying, that where the economical and political conditions of countries are touched upon in the following work, the remarks are less her own than elsewhere.

33 William Wordsworth, *Guide to the Lakes*, ed. Ernest de Sélincourt (London: Frances Lincoln, 2004), p. 95. Hereafter abbreviated to Wordsworth, *Guide* with page numbers given in parenthesis.

34 This remained a popular mode of ascending Skiddaw for female travellers for more than a century and anxieties about the journey clearly lessened as ascents became more common; Martineau notes in her 1855 *Guide* that 'The ascent of Skiddaw is easy, even for ladies, who have only to sit on their ponies to find themselves at the top, after a ride of six miles'. Harriet Martineau, *A Complete Guide to the English Lakes* (Garnett: Windermere, Westmorland, 1855), p. 90. In his popular guide to the Lakes, first issued in 1880 and reprinted throughout the early years of the twentieth century, Baddeley still provides the cost of both guide and pony hire for the visitor. M. J. B. Baddeley, *The English Lake District* (Dulau: London, 1906), p. 229.

35 Radcliffe's route is closer to that of Gray than of West and though she approaches the Lakes from a different direction to Gray (he arrives from the Eden Valley in the East and arrives first at Penrith, whilst she approaches from the South and travels up from Lancaster to Kendal) and though Radcliffe's tour is more extensive (Gray then travels straight back from Keswick, heading south to Kendal and Lancaster, leaving out Coniston and its environs altogether) both writers leave the Lakes by travelling across the sands of Morecambe Bay and the central section of their journey follows a similar pattern of trips undertaken from Keswick.

36 William Roberts, 'Commentary', *Thomas Gray's Journal of his Visit to the Lake District in October 1769*, ed. William Roberts (Liverpool: Liverpool University Press, 2001), p. 42. The Radcliffes do though sometimes elect for the smaller inns rather than the most popular tourist venues (see for example their choice of the King's Arms at Patterdale over the principal village inn of the period) so they may well have chosen The George, the town's oldest coaching inn, as an alternative.

37 Grevel Lindop, *A Literary Guide to the Lake District* (Wilmslow: Sigma Press, 2005), p. 129. In the same year in which the Radcliffes visited, Derwentwater received another literary put-down in a poem by Richard Payne Knight, in which he notes that 'Keswick's favoured pool / Is made the theme of ev'ry wandering fool' (cited in Lindop, p. 130).

38 *Selected Letters of John Keats*, ed. Grant F. Scott, revised edn. (Cambridge, Massachusetts: Harvard University Press, 2002), p. 131. Hereafter referred to as *Selected Letters of John Keats*.

39 Thurston-Lake or Thurstonmere was the former name for Coniston Water and was still widely used in the late eighteenth-century.

40 James Plumptre, *The Lakers: A Comic Opera, in Three Acts* (Oxford: Woodstock Books, 1990), p. 18.

41 Angela Jones, 'Romantic Women Travel Writers and the Representation of Everyday Experience', *Women's Studies* 26 (1997), 497-521 (p. 510).

42 For further discussion of this trope in women's writing of the period see Penny Bradshaw, 'Dystopian Futures: Time Travel and Millenarian Visions in the poetry of Anna Barbauld and Charlotte Smith', *Romanticism on the Net*, 21 (February 2001) [http://www.erudit.org/revue/ron/2001/v/n21/005959ar.html].

43 Helen Maria Williams, *Letters Written in France in the Summer of 1790* (London: Cadell, 1794), pp. 22-4.

44 See for example Wordsworth's portrayal of Michael in his poem of the same name and his account of the shepherds in Book 8 of *The Prelude*: 'Man free, man working for himself, with choice / Of time, and place, and objects'. *William Wordsworth: The Major Works*, ed. Stephen Gill (Oxford: Oxford University Press, 2008), p. 490, ll. 152-3. Hereafter abbreviated to Wordsworth, *Major Works*.

45 Radcliffe's fellow novelist Charlotte Smith is another important forerunner to Wordsworth in this respect since her Grasmere-based novel, *Ethelinde* also depicts a vision of peaceful rural solitary living in the Lakes.

46 Radcliffe in fact believes that she is in the hamlet of Martindale at this point but is clearly mistaken as she and her husband were wandering along the banks of Haweswater in the area known as Mardale Green or Mardale Common. The confusion probably arises because of a lack of exact dimensions and indeed downright cartographical inaccuracies on the early maps of the region. West's map of 1784 is deeply confusing since it depicts Ullswater as lying to the north-east of Haweswater, whereas in fact Ullswater lies to the north-west of Haweswater; West's map does not mention Mardale at all but does depict Martindale forest as lying between the two lakes. It seems that with the limited cartographical assistance available to them, the Radcliffes believed themselves to be in the area known as Martindale. Their confusion is compounded by peculiarities of local dialect with which Radcliffe had already struggled; she refers to the 'chapel of Martindale, spoken by the country people Mardale'. Only a couple of pages prior to this Radcliffe had reflected on the 'danger of wandering in these regions without a guide' and losing your way, and we should not underestimate the difficulty experienced by early tourists in navigating around this unknown and fairly inhospitable region without a guide and supported only with the limited maps of the period.

47 For a detailed account of the Wordsworths' early plans to settle together in rural retirement see chapter two of Newlyn. The parallels between the Wordsworths' fantasies for a life of seclusion in a cottage in the Lakes and Radcliffe's own vision are very marked and at one point Dorothy even imagines herself and her brother living in a 'little Parsonage'. *The Letters of Dorothy and William Wordsworth: The Early Years, 1787-1805,* ed. Ernest de Sélincourt (Oxford: Clarendon Press, 1967), p. 88.

48 Accounts of an ascent of Skiddaw prior to *Observations* appear in William Hutchinson's *An Excursion to the Lakes* (1774), Adam Walker's *A Tour from London*

to the Lakes (1792) and Joseph Budworth's *A Fortnight's Ramble to the Lakes* (1792). Of these, the most interesting account is that of Hutchinson who offers a vivid and colourful description of the storm which breaks out whilst he and his party are at the top of Skiddaw. The fact that it is Radcliffe's account which comes to be absorbed into the main itinerary guide of the period though clearly indicates the uniqueness and appeal of her narrative over and above these other earlier descriptions. Bainbridge notes that 'As early as 1798 this nascent summit fever had become a target for satire' and quotes the lines from James Plumptre's play, *The Lakers*, in which Veronica, the novelist, plans an ascent of Skiddaw by pony; Plumptre's satirical reference is though primarily targeted at Radcliffe's own account of the Lakes, and while descriptions of ascents of Skiddaw had been included in a small number of earlier guides, none of these reached the same kind of readership as Radcliffe's account once this had been incorporated into the ubiquitous West from 1796 onwards. There are some grounds for suggesting therefore that it is Radcliffe's very well-known and popular account of the ascent of Skiddaw which fuelled the early 'summit fever' described by Bainbridge. See Simon Bainbridge, 'Romantic Writers and Mountaineering', *Romanticism* 18:1 (2012), 1-15 (p. 4).

49 Tim Fulford, *The Late Poetry of the Lake Poets: Romanticism Revisited* (Cambridge: Cambridge University Press, 2013), p. 30.

50 Norman Nicholson, *The Lakers: The Adventures of the First Tourists* (London: Robert Hale, 1955), p. 83.

51 *The Letters of William and Dorothy Wordsworth: The Middle Years, 1806-1820*, ed. Ernest de Sélincourt, 2 vols (Oxford: Clarendon Press, 1969-70), II, p. 232.

52 Duncan Wu, *Wordsworth's Reading 1770-1799* (Cambridge: Cambridge University Press, 1993), p. 115.

53 See Bicknell, p. 36.

54 In the introduction to Wordsworth's prose *Guide to the Lakes* for example, Ernest de Sélincourt specifically cites Radcliffe's tour amongst those 'predecessors' about whom Wordsworth gallantly stays silent 'where he must have felt so much', a comment which clearly indicates a belief on de Sélincourt's part that Wordsworth must have been familiar with *Observations*. Ernest de Sélincourt, 'Introduction' to William Wordsworth, *Guide to the Lakes*, ed. Ernest de Sélincourt (London: Frances Lincoln, 2004), pp. ix-xxiv (p. xvi).

55 *Unpublished Letters of Samuel Taylor Coleridge*, ed. Earl Leslie Griggs, 2 vols (London: Constable, 1932), II, p. 407.

56 *Collected Letters of Samuel Taylor Coleridge*, ed. Earl Leslie Griggs vol. 1: 1785-1800 (Oxford: Clarendon Press, 1956), p. 183.

57 See Penny Bradshaw, 'Romantic Poetic Identity and the English Lake District', *Transactions of the Cumberland and Westmorland Antiquarian and Archaeological Society,* 11 (2011), 65-80.

58 Richard Holmes, *Coleridge: Early Visions* (London: Penguin, 1989), p. 287.

59 *Samuel Taylor Coleridge: The Complete Poems*, ed. William Keach (London: Penguin, 2004), pp. 196-7.

60 As in the case of Wordsworth, some traces of a Radcliffean influence have been identified by contemporary critics in relation to Coleridge's work, but specifically in relation to her novels. Norton notes that he 'incorporated many Gothic stage

properties from Radcliffe's work into his own' and identifies the reference to the 'Mad Lutanist' in *Dejection: An Ode* as a 'direct and important allusion to Signora Laurentini (mad Sister Agnes), whose mysterious music in the grounds of the Château-le-Blanc persuades everyone that it is haunted'; Norton suggests that 'there seems little doubt that he is indebted to his predecessor's development of the imagery of grief and the sighing of the wind' but does not go on to make the connection between this trope and Radcliffe's handling of similar imagery in relation to Lake District contexts specifically (p. 251).

61 Wu cites Robert Woof's claim that 'The smugglers no doubt were fed into Wordsworth's imagination by certain situations in Mrs. Radcliffe's *Romance of the Forest*' (Wu, p.115) and Robert Osborn, in the introduction to the Cornell edition of *The Borderers*, seems to rather reluctantly acknowledge a specific link between the two texts, suggesting that the 'black Appearance' in the play 'is wholly explicable in rational terms, and so belongs to the tradition of Ann Radcliffe's popular *Romance of the Forest* (1791)'; Osborn goes on to quickly minimise the idea of influence by suggesting that 'Mrs. Radcliffe's apparitions are designed to satisfy her audience's desire for spectral sensationalism without offending their rationalist sensibilities. Wordsworth's concern is to demonstrate the psychological susceptibility of his protagonist'– a comment which effectively situates Radcliffe as a tawdry populist author governed by market forces and Wordsworth as an experimental and complex playwright, neither of which is entirely borne out by the two texts in question. Though Osborn flags the influence of eighteenth-century Gothic traditions on *The Borderers* more broadly, he makes no further mention of more extensive influence from the key exponent of this genre. Yet alongside the imagery, several elements of the plot (the scene of planned murder at a ruined castle on a stormy night, mistaken parenthood and so forth) are very typical of Radcliffe. In the 'literary sources influencing Wordsworth's treatment of [the Lakes] landscape' specifically, Osborn only cites male-authored texts: Gilpin's *Observations*, Hutchinson's *Excursion* (1774), West's *Guide* (1778), and Clarke's *Survey* (1787). See 'Introduction', *The Borderers by William Wordsworth* (Ithaca and London: Cornell University Press, 1982), pp. 3-39 (p. 21 and p. 19).

62 John Harrington Smith, 'Genesis of *The Borderers*', *PMLA*, 49:3 (September 1934), 922-30 (p. 925).

63 Thomas De Quincey, *The Works of Thomas De Quincey*, ed Grevel Lindop, 2 vols (London: Pickering and Chatto, 2000), II, p. 146.

64 Though Keats sets out on the tour as a devotee of Wordsworth, his experiences in the North challenged his earlier perceptions of both the Lakes and the Wordsworthian poetic model and it is following this trip that he formulates his famous critique of the 'wordsworthian or egotistical sublime' (*Selected Letters of John Keats*, p. 194) and begins to shape his own, very different, model of poetic identity. See Bradshaw (2011).

65 Eliza Lynn Linton, *The Lake Country* (London: Smith, Elder and Co, 1864), p. ix.

66 H. D. Rawnsley, *Literary Associations of the English Lakes,* 2 vols (Glasgow: MacLehose and Sons, 1894), I, p. 160.

67 Terry Castle, 'The Spectralization of the Other in the *Mysteries of Udolpho*,' in *The New Eighteenth-Century*, ed. Felicity Nussbaum and Laura Brown (Routledge:

New York, 1987), pp. 231-53 (p. 232).

68 For a reading of Keats's comments on Radcliffe as a sign of his own cultural anxieties see Mellor, p. 183 and Norton, p. 253.

Suggestions for Further Reading

Peter Bicknell, *The Picturesque Scenery of the Lake District, 1752-1855* (1990).

Elizabeth A. Bohls, *Women Travel Writers and the Language of Aesthetics, 1716-1818* (Cambridge: Cambridge University Press, 1995).

George Decker, *The Fictions of Romantic Tourism: Radcliffe, Scott, and Mary Shelley* (Redwood: Stanford University Press, 2004).

Angela D. Jones, 'Romantic Women Travel Writers and the Representation of Everyday Experience', *Women's Studies* 26 (1997), 497-521.

Zoë Kingsley, *Women Writing the Home Tour, 1682-1812* (Aldershot: Ashgate, 2008).

Ingrid Kuczynski, 'Reading a Landscape: Ann Radcliffe's *A Journey Made in the Summer of 1794, Through Holland and the Western Frontier of Germany, With a Return Down the Rhine* (1795)', in *British Romantics as Readers: Intertextualities, Maps of Misreading, Reinterpretations*, ed. Michael Gassenmeier *et al* (Heidelberg: Universitätsverlag C. Winter, 1998), pp. 241-257.

Dorothy McMillan, 'The Secret of Ann Radcliffe's English Travels', in *Romantic Geographies: Discourses of Travel 1775-1844*, ed. Amanda Gilroy (Manchester: Manchester University Press, 2000), pp. 51-67.

Robert Miles, *Ann Radcliffe: the Great Enchantress* (Manchester: Manchester UP, 1995).

Jeanne Moskal, 'Ann Radcliffe's Lake District', *The Wordsworth Circle* 31: 1 (Winter 2000), 56-62.

Rictor Norton, *Mistress of Udolpho: The Life of Ann Radcliffe* (London and New York: Leicester University Press, 1999).

Dale Townshend and Angela Wright (eds), *Ann Radcliffe, Romanticism and the Gothic* (Cambridge: Cambridge University Press, 2014).

~~~

LANCASTER[1]

F ROM MANCHESTER to Lancaster the road leads through a pleasant and populous country, which rises gradually as it approaches the huge hills we had noticed in the distance from the brow of Cheshire, and whose attitudes now resembled those of the Rheingau as seen from Mentz.[2] From some moors on this side of Lancaster the prospects open very extensively over a rich tract fading into blue ridges; while, on the left, long lines of distant sea appear, every now and then, over the dark woods of the shore, with vessels sailing as if on their summits. But the view from a hill descending to Lancaster is pre-eminent for grandeur, and comprehends an extent of sea and land, and a union of the sublime in both, which we have never seen equalled. In the green vale of the Lune below lies the town, spreading up the side of a round hill overtopped by the old towers of the castle and the church. Beyond, over a ridge of gentle heights, which bind the west side of the vale, the noble inlet of the sea, that flows upon the Ulverston and Lancaster sands, is seen at the feet of an amphitheatre formed by nearly all the mountains of the Lakes; an exhibition of alpine grandeur, both in form and colouring, which, with the extent of water below, compose a scenery perhaps faintly rivalling that of the Lake of Geneva. To the south and west, the Irish Channel finishes the view.

The antient town and castle of Lancaster have been so often and so well described, that little remains to be said of them. To the latter considerable additions are building in the Gothic style, which, when time shall have shaded the stone, will harmonize well with the venerable towers and gate-house of the old structure. From a turret rising over the leads of the castle, called John o' Gaunt's Chair, the prospect is still finer than from the terrace of the church-yard below. Overlooking the Lune and its green slopes, the eye ranges to the bay of the sea beyond, and to the Cumberland and Lancashire mountains. On an island near the extremity of the peninsula of Low Furness, the double point of Peel Castle starts up from the sea, but is so distant that it resembles a forked rock. This peninsula, which separates the bay of Ulverston from the Irish Channel, swells gradually into a pointed mountain called Blackcomb, thirty miles from Lancaster, the first in the amphitheatre, that binds the bay. Hence a range of lower, but more broken and forked summits, extends northward to the fells of High Furness, rolled behind each other, huge, towering and dark; then, higher still, Langdale Pikes, with a confusion of other fells, that crown the head of Windermere and retire towards Keswick, whose gigantic mountains, Helvellyn and Saddleback, are, however, sunk in distance below the horizon of the nearer ones. The top of Skiddaw may be discerned when the air is clear, but it is too far off to appear with dignity. From Windermere-Fells the heights soften towards the Vale of Lonsdale, on the east side of which Ingleborough, a mountain in Craven, rears his rugged front, the loftiest and most majestic in the scene. The nearer country, from this point of the landscape, is intersected with cultivated hills, between which the Lune winds its bright but shallow stream, falling over a weir and passing under a very handsome stone bridge at the entrance of the town, in its progress towards the sea. A ridge of rocky eminences shelters Lancaster on the east, whence they decline into the low and uninteresting country, that stretches to the Channel.

The appearance of the northern Fells is ever changing with the weather and shifting lights. Sometimes they resemble those evening clouds on the horizon, that catch the last gleams of the sun; at others, wrapt in dark mist, they are only faintly traced, and seem like stormy vapours rising from the sea. But in a bright day their appearance is beautiful; then, their grand outlines are distinctly drawn upon the sky, a vision of Alps; the rugged sides are faintly marked with light and shadow, with wood and rock, and here and there a cluster of white cottages, or farms and hamlets, gleam at their feet along the water's edge. Over the whole landscape is then drawn a softening azure, or sometimes a purple hue, exquisitely lovely, while the sea below reflects a brighter tint of blue.

FROM LANCASTER TO KENDAL

L EAVING LANCASTER, we wound along the southern brow of the vale of the Lune, which there serpentizes among meadows, and is soon after shut up between steep shrubby banks. From the heights we had some fine retrospects of Lancaster and the distant sea; but, about three miles from the town, the hills open forward to a view as much distinguished by the notice of Mr. Gray, as by its own charms.[3] We here looked down over a woody and finely broken fore-ground upon the Lune and the vale of Lonsdale, undulating in richly cultivated slopes, with Ingleborough, for the back-ground, bearing its bold promontory on high, the very crown and paragon of the landscape. To the west, the vale winds from sight among smoother hills; and the gracefully falling line of a mountain, on the left, forms, with the wooded heights, on the right, a kind of frame for the distant picture.

The road now turned into the sweetly retired vale of Caton, and by the village church-yard, in which there is not a single gravestone, to Hornby, a small straggling town, delightfully seated near the entrance of the vale of Lonsdale. Its thin toppling castle is seen among wood, at a considerable distance, with a dark hill rising over it. What remains of the old edifice is a square grey building, with a slender watch-tower, rising in one corner, like a feather in a hat, which joins the modern mansion of white stone, and gives it a singular appearance, by seeming to start from the centre of its roof.

In front, a steep lawn descends between avenues of old wood, and the park extends along the skirts of the craggy hill, that towers above. At its foot, is a good stone bridge over the Wenning, now shrunk in its pebbly bed, and, further on, near the castle, the church, shewing a handsome octagonal tower, crowned with battlements. The road then becomes extremely interesting, and, at Melling, a village on a brow some miles further, the view opens over the whole vale of Lonsdale. The eye now passes, beneath the arching foliage of some trees in the fore-ground, to the sweeping valley, where meadows of the most vivid green and dark woods, with white cottages and villages peeping from among them, mingle with surprising richness, and undulate from either bank of the Lune to the feet of hills. Ingleborough, rising from elegantly swelling ground, overlooked this enchanting vale, on the right, clouds rolling along its broken top, like smoke from a cauldron, and its hoary tint forming a boundary to the soft verdure and rich woodlands of the slopes, at its feet. The perspective was terminated by the tall peeping heads of the Westmoreland fells, the nearer ones tinged with faintest purple, the more distant with light azure; and this is the general boundary to a scene, in the midst of which, enclosed between nearer and lower hills, lies the vale of Lonsdale, of a character mild, delicate and reposing, like the countenance of a Madonna.

Descending Melling brow, and winding among the perpetually changing scenery of the valley, we approached Ingleborough; and it was interesting to observe the lines of its bolder features gradually strengthening, and the shadowy markings of its minuter ones becoming more distinct, as we advanced. Rock and grey crags looked out from the heath, on every side; but its form on each was very different. Towards Lonsdale, the mountain is bold and majestic, rising in abrupt and broken precipices, and often impending, till, at the summit, it suddenly becomes flat, and is level for nearly a mile, whence it descends, in a long gradual ridge, to Craven in Yorkshire. In summer, some festivities are annually celebrated on this top, and the country people, as they 'drink the freshness of the mountain breeze,'* look over the wild moorlands of Yorkshire, the rich vales of Lancashire, and to the sublime mountains of Westmoreland.[4]

Crossing a small bridge, we turned from Ingleborough, and passed very near the antient walls of Thirlham Castle, little of which is now remaining.[5] The ruin is on a green broken knoll, one side of which is darkened with brush-wood and dwarf-oak. Cattle were reposing in the shade, on the bank of a rivulet, that rippled through what was formerly the castle ditch. A few old trees waved over what was once a tower, now covered with ivy.

Some miles further, we crossed the Leck, a shrunk and desolate stream, nearly choked with pebbles, winding in a deep rocky glen, where trees and shrubs marked the winter boundary of the waters. Our road, mounting a green eminence of the opposite bank, on which stands Overborough, the handsome modern mansion of Mr. Fenwick, wound between plantations and meadows, painted with yellow and purple flowers, like those of spring.[6] As we passed through their gentle slopes, we had, now and then, sweet views between the foliage, on the left, into the vale of Lonsdale, now contracting in its course, and winding into ruder scenery. Among these catches, the best picture was, perhaps, where the white town of Kirby Lonsdale shelves along the opposite bank, having rough heathy hills immediately above it, and, below, a venerable Gothic bridge over the Lune, rising in tall arches, like an antient aqueduct; its grey tint agreeing well with the silvery lightness of the water and the green shades, that flourished from the steep margin over the abutments.[7]

The view from this bridge, too, was beautiful. The river, foaming below among masses of dark rock, variegated with light tints of grey, as if touched by the painter's pencil, withdrew towards the south in a straight channel, with the woods of Overborough on the left. The vale, dilating, opened a long perspective to Ingleborough and many blue mountains more distant, with all the little villages we had passed, glittering on the intervening eminences. The colouring of some low hills, on the right, was particularly beautiful, long shades of wood being overtopped with brown heath, while, below, meadows of soft verdure fell gently towards the river bank.

*   Mrs. Barbauld

Engraving of Kirkby Lonsdale Bridge, pub. by Harding, 1801

Kirby Lonsdale, a neat little town, commanding the whole vale, is on the western steep. We staid two hours at it, gratified by witnessing, at the first inn we reached, the abundance of the country and the goodwill of the people. In times, when the prices of necessary articles are increasing with the taste for all unnecessary display, instances of cheapness may be to persons of small incomes something more than mere physical treasures; they have a moral value in contributing to independence of mind.

Here we had an early and, as it afterwards appeared, a very exaggerated specimen of the dialect of the country. A woman talked, for five minutes, against our window, of whose conversation we could understand scarcely a word. Soon after, a boy replied to a question, '*I do na ken,*' and '*gang*' was presently the common word for go; symptoms of nearness to a country, which we did not approach, without delighting to enumerate the instances of genius and worth, that adorn it.

Leaving Kirby-Lonsdale by the Kendal road, we mounted a steep hill, and, looking back from its summit upon the whole vale of Lonsdale, perceived ourselves to be in the mid-way between beauty and desolation, so enchanting was the retrospect and so wild and dreary the prospect. From the neighbourhood of Caton to Kirby the ride was superior, for elegant beauty, to any we had passed; this from Kirby to Kendal is of a character distinctly opposite. After losing sight of the vale, the road lies, for nearly the whole distance, over moors and perpetually succeeding hills, thinly covered with dark purple heath flowers, of which the most distant seemed black. The dreariness of the scene was increased by a heavy rain and by the slowness of our progress, jostling amongst coal carts, for ten miles of rugged ground. The views over the Westmoreland mountains were, however, not entirely obscured; their vast ridges were visible in the horizon to the north and west, line over line, frequently in five or six ranges. Sometimes the intersecting mountains opened to others beyond, that fell in deep and abrupt precipices, their profiles drawing towards a point below and seeming to sink in a bottomless abyss.

On our way over these wilds, parts of which are called Endmoor and Cowbrows, we overtook only long trains of coal carts, and, after ten miles of bleak mountain road, began to desire a temporary home, somewhat sooner than we perceived Kendal, white-smoking in the dark vale. As we approached, the outlines of its ruinous castle were just distinguishable through the gloom, scattered in masses over the top of a small round hill, on the right. At the entrance of the town, the river Kent dashed in foam down a weir; beyond it, on a green slope, the gothic tower of the church was half hid by a cluster of dark trees; gray fells glimmered in the distance.

We were lodged at another excellent inn, and, the next morning, walked over the town, which has an air of trade mingled with that of antiquity. Its history has been given in other places, and we are not able to discuss the doubt, whether it was the Roman *Brocanonacio*, or not.[8] The manufacture of cloth, which our statute books testify to have existed as early as the reign, in which *Falstaff* is made to allude to it, appears to be still in vigour, for the town is surrounded, towards the river, with dying grounds.[9] We saw, however, no shades of 'Kendal green,' or, indeed, any but bright scarlet.

The church is remarkable for three chapels, memorials of the antient dignity of three neighbouring families, the Bellinghams, Stricklands and Parrs.[10] These are inclosures, on each side of the altar, differing from pews chiefly in being large enough to contain tombs. Mr. Gray noticed them minutely in the year 1769. They were then probably entire; but the wainscot or railing, which divided the chapel of the Parrs from the aisle, is now gone. Of two stone tombs in it one is inclosed with modern railing, and there are many remnants of painted arms on the adjoining windows. The chapel of the Stricklands, which is between this and the altar, is separated from the church aisle by a solid wainscot, to the height of four feet, and after that by a wooden railing with broken filigree ornaments. That of the Bellinghams contains an antient tomb, of which the brass plates, that bore inscriptions and arms, are now gone, but some traces of the latter remain in plaistered stone at the side. Over it, are the fragments of an helmet, and, in the roof, those of armorial bearings, carved in wood. On a pillar, near this, is an inscription, almost obliterated, in which the following words may yet be traced:

> Dame Thomasim Thornburgh
> Wiffe of Sir William Thornburgh Knyght
> Daughter of Sir Robert Bellingham
> Gentle Knyght: the ellventhe of August
> On thousand fyve hundreth eightie too.

The Saxon has been so strongly engrafted on our language, that, in reading old inscriptions, especially those, which are likely to have been spelt, according to the pronunciation, one is frequently reminded by antient English words of the modern German synonyms. A German of the present day would say for eleven, eilf, pronounced long like eilve, and for five, funf, pronounced like fuynf.

Over the chief seat in the old pew of the Bellinghams is a brass plate, engraved with the figure of a man in armour, and, on each side of it, a brass escutcheon, of which that on the right has a motto thus spelled *Ains. y L'est*.[11] Under the figure is the following inscription, also cut in brass:

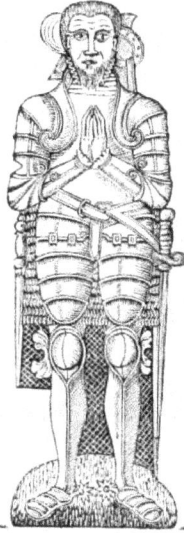

Engraving of the brass plate in Kendal Church, from C. Nicholson, Annals of Kendal, *1832*

> Heer lyeth the bodye of Alan Bellingham esquier who maryed Catheryan daughter of Anthonye Ducket esquier by whom he had no children after whose decease he maryed Dorothie daughter of Thomas Sanford esquier of whom he had — sonnes & eight daughters, of which five sonnes & 7daughters with the said Dorothie ar yeat lyving, he was threscore and one yares of age & dyed ye 7 of Maye Ao dni 1577.

The correctness of inserting the unpronounced consonants in the words Eight and Daughters, notwithstanding the varieties of the other orthography in this inscription, is a proof of the universality of the Saxon mode of spelling, with great abundance and even waste of letters; a mode, which is so incorporated with our language, that those, who are for dispensing with it in some instances, as in the final k in 'publick' and other words, should consider what a general change they have to effect, or what partial incongruities they must submit to.

Kendal is built on the lower steeps of a hill, that towers over the principal street, and bears on one of its brows a testimony to the independence of the inhabitants, an obelisk dedicated to liberty and to the memory of the Revolution in 1688.[12] At a time, when the memory of that revolution is reviled, and the praises of liberty itself endeavoured to be suppressed by the artifice of imputing to it the crimes of anarchy, it was impossible to omit any act of veneration to the blessings of this event. Being thus led to ascend the hill, we had a view of the country, over which it presides; a scene simple, great and free as the spirit revered amidst it.

FROM KENDAL TO BAMPTON AND HAWESWATER

O F TWO ROADS from Kendal to Bampton one is through Long Sleddale, the other over Shapfell, the king of the Westmoreland mountains; of which routes the last is the most interesting for simple sublimity, leading through the heart of the wildest tracts and opening to such vast highland scenery as even Derbyshire cannot shew. We left Kendal by this road, and from a very old, ruinous bridge had a full view of the castle, stretching its dark walls and broken towers round the head of a green hill, to the southward of the town. These reliques are, however, too far separated by the decay of large masses of the original edifice, and contain little that is individually picturesque.

The road now lay through shady lanes and over undulating, but gradually ascending ground, from whence were pleasant views of the valley, with now and then a break in the hills, on the left, opening to a glimpse of the distant fells towards Windermere, gray and of more pointed form than any we had yet seen; for hitherto the mountains, though of huge outline, were not so broken, or alpine in their summits as to strike the fancy with surprize. After about three miles, a very steep hill shuts up the vale to the North, and from a gray rock, near the summit, called Stone-cragg, the prospect opens over the vale of Kendal with great dignity and beauty. Its form from hence seems nearly circular; the hills spread round it, and sweep with easy lines into the bottom, green nearly to their summits, where no fantastic points bend over it, though rock frequently mingles with the heath. The castle, or its low green hill, looked well, nearly in the centre of the landscape, with Kendal and its mountain, on the right. Far to the south, were the groves of Leven's park, almost the only wood in the scene, and, over the heights beyond, blue hills bounded the horizon. On the west, an opening in the near steeps discovered clusters of huge and broken fells, while other breaks, on the east, shewed long ridges stretching towards the south. Nearer us and to the northward, the hills rose dark and awful, crowding over and intersecting each other in long and abrupt lines, heath and crag their only furniture.

The rough knolls around us and the dark mountain above gave force to the verdant beauty and tranquillity of the vale below, and seemed especially to shelter from the storms of the north some white farms and cottages, scattered among enclosures in the hollows. Soon after reaching the summit of the mountain itself

'A vale appear'd below, a deep retir'd abode,'[13]

and we looked down on the left into Long Sleddale, a little scene of exquisite beauty, surrounded with images of greatness. This narrow vale, or glen, shewed a level of the brightest verdure, with a few cottages scattered among groves, enclosed by dark fells, that rose steeply, yet gracefully, and, at their summits, bent forward in masses of shattered rock. An hugely pointed mountain, called Keintmoor-head, shuts up this sweet scene to the north, rising in a sudden precipice from the vale, and heightening, by barren and gloomy steeps, the miniature beauty, that glowed at its feet. Two mountains, called Whiteside and Potter's-fell, screen the perspective; Stone-crag is at the southern end, fronting Keintmoor-head. The vale, seen beyond the broken ground we were upon, formed a landscape of, perhaps, unexampled variety and grace of colouring; the tender green of the lowland, the darker verdure of the woods ascending the mountains, the brown rough heath above them, and the impending crags over all, exhibit their numerous shades, within a space not more than two miles long, or half a mile in breadth.

From the right of our road another valley extended, whose character is that of simple sublimity, unmixed with any tint of beauty. The vast, yet narrow perspective sweeps in ridges of mountains, huge, barren and brown, point beyond point, the highest of which, Howgill-fell, gives its name to the whole district, in which not a wood, a village, or a farm appeared to cheer the long vista. A shepherd boy told us the names of almost all the heights within the horizon, and we are sorry not to have written them, for the names of mountains are seldom compounded of modern, or trivial denominations, and frequently are somewhat descriptive of their prototypes. He informed us also, that we should go over eight miles of Shap-fell, without seeing a house; and soon after, at Haw's-foot, we took leave of the last on the road, entering then a close valley, surrounded by stupendous mountains of heath and rock, more towering and abrupt than those, that had appeared in moorlands on the other side of Kendal. A stream, rolling in its rocky channel, and crossing the road under a rude bridge, was all that broke the solitary silence, or gave animation to the view, except the flocks, that hung upon the precipices, and which, at that height, were scarcely distinguishable from the grey round stones, thickly starting out from the heathy steeps. The Highlands of Scotland could scarcely have offered to Ossian more images of simple greatness, or more circumstances for melancholy inspiration.[14] Dark glens and fells, the mossy stone, the lonely blast, descending on the valley, the roar of distant torrents every where occurred; and to the bard the 'song of spirits' would have swelled with these sounds, and their fleeting forms have appeared in the clouds, that frequently floated along the mountain tops.

The road, now ascending Shap-fell, alternately climbed the steeps and sunk among the hollows of this sovereign mountain, which gives its name to all the surrounding hills; and, during an ascent of four miles, we watched every form and attitude of the features, which composed this vast scenery. Sometimes we looked from a precipice into deep vallies, varied only with shades of heath, with the rude summer hut of the shepherd, or by streams accumulating into torrents; and, at others, caught long prospects over high lands as huge and wild as the nearer ones, which partially intercepted them.

The flocks in this high region are so seldom disturbed by the footsteps of man, that they have not learned to fear him; they continued to graze within a few feet of the carriage, or looked quietly at it, seeming to consider these mountains as their own.

Near the summit of the road, though not of the hill, a retrospective glance gave us a long view over the fells, and of a rich distance towards Lancaster, rising into blue hills, which admitted glimpses of sparkling sea in the bay beyond. This gay perspective, lighted up by a gleam of sunshine, and viewed between the brown lines of the nearer mountains, shewed like the miniature painting of a landscape, illuminated beyond a darkened fore-ground.

At the point of every steep, as we ascended, the air seemed to become thinner, and, at the northern summit of Shap-fell, which we reached after nearly two hours' toil, the wind blew with piercing intenseness, making it difficult to remain as long as was due to our admiration of the prospect. The scene of mountains, which burst upon us, can be compared only to the multitudinous waves of the sea. On the northern, western and eastern scope of the horizon rose vast ridges of heights, their broken lines sometimes appearing in seven or eight successive ranges, though shewing nothing either fantastic or peaked in their forms. The autumnal lights, gleaming on their sides, or shadows sweeping in dark lines along them, produced a very sublime effect; while summits more remote were often misty with the streaming shower, and others glittered in the partial rays, or were coloured with the mild azure of distance. The greater tract of the intervening hills and Shap-fell itself were, at this time, darkened with clouds, while Fancy, awed by the gloom, imaged the genius of Westmoreland brooding over it and directing the scowling storm.

A descent of nearly four miles brought us to Shap, a straggling village, lying on the side of a bleak hill, feebly sheltered by clumps of trees. Here, leaving the moorlands, we were glad to find ourselves again where 'bells have knolled to church,' and in the midst of civilized, though simple life.[15] After a short rest, at a cleanly little inn, we proceeded towards Bampton, a village five miles further in a vale, to which it gives its name, and one mile from Haweswater, the lake, that invited us to it. As the road advanced, the fells of this lake fronted it, and, closing over the southern end of Bampton vale, were the most interesting objects in the view. They were of a character very different from any yet seen; tall, rocky, and of more broken and pointed form. Among them was the high blue peak, called Kidstowpike; the broader ridge of Wallow-crag; a round and still loftier mountain—Ikolm-moor, beyond, and, further yet, other ranges of peaked summits, that overlook Ullswater.

In a hollow on the left of the road, called the Vale of Magdalene, are the ruins of Shap-abbey, built in the reign of John, of which little now appears except a tower with pointed windows. The situation is deeply secluded, and the gloom of the surrounding mountains may have accorded well with monastic melancholy.

Proceeding towards Bampton we had a momentary peep into Haweswater, sunk deep among black and haggard rocks, and overtopped by the towering fells before named, whose summits were involved in tempest, till the sun, suddenly breaking out from under clouds, threw a watery gleam aslant the broken top of Kidstowpike; and his rays, struggling with the shower, produced a fine effect of light, opposed to the gloom, that wrapt Ickolm-moor and other huge mountains.

We soon after looked down from the heights of Bampton upon its open vale, checkered with corn and meadows, among which the slender

Lowther wound its way from Haweswater to the vale of Eden, crossing that of Bampton to the north. The hills, enriched here and there with hanging woods and seats, were cultivated nearly to their summits, except where in the south the rude heights of Haweswater almost excluded the lake and shut up the valley. Immediately below us Bampton-grange lay along the skirt of the hill, and crossed the Lowther, a grey, rambling and antient village, to which we descended among rough common, darkened by plantations of fir, and between corn enclosures.

The interruption, which inclosed waters and pathless mountains give to the intercourse and business of ordinary life, renders the district, that contains the lakes of Lancashire, Westmoreland and Cumberland, more thinly inhabited than is due to the healthiness of the climate and, perhaps, to the richness of the vallies. The roads are always difficult from their steepness, and in winter are greatly obstructed by snow. That over Shap-fell to Kendal was, some years since, entirely impassable, till the inhabitants of a few scattered towns subscribed thirty pounds, and a way was cut wide enough for one horse, but so deep, that the snow was, on each side, above the rider's head. It is not in this age of communication and intelligence, that any person will be credulously eager to suppose the inhabitants of one part of the island considerably or generally distinguished in their characters from those of another; yet, perhaps, none can immerge themselves in this country of the lakes, without being struck by the superior simplicity and modesty of the people. Secluded from great towns and from examples of selfish splendour, their minds seem to act freely in the sphere of their own affairs, without interruption from envy or triumph, as to those of others. They are obliging, without servility, and plain but not rude, so that, when, in accosting you, they omit the customary appellations, you perceive it to be the familiarity of kindness, not of disrespect; and they do not bend with meanness, or hypocrisy, but shew an independent well meaning, without obtrusiveness and without the hope of more than ordinary gain.

Their views of profit from strangers are, indeed, more limited than we could have believed, before witnessing it. The servants at the little inns confess themselves by their manner of receiving what you give, to be almost as much surprised as pleased. A boy, who had opened four or five gates for us between Shap and Bampton, blushed when we called to him to have some halfpence; and it frequently happened, that persons, who had looked at the harness, or rendered some little services of that sort on the road, passed on, before anything could be offered them. The confusion of others, on being paid, induced us to suppose, at first, that enough had not been given; but we were soon informed, that nothing was expected.

The inns, as here at Bampton, are frequently humble; and those, who are disposed to clamour for luxuries, as if there was a crime in not being able to supply them, may confound a simple people, and be themselves greatly discontented, before they go. But those, who will be satisfied with comforts, and think the experience of integrity, carefulness and goodwill is itself a luxury, will be glad to have stopped at Bampton and at several other little villages, where there is some sort of preparation for travellers.

Nor is this secluded spot without provision for the mind. A beneficed grammar school receives the children of the inhabitants, and sends, we believe, some to an University. Bishop Gibson received his education at it.[16] Bishop Law, who was born at Bampton, went daily across one, or two of the rudest fells on the lake to another school, at Martindale;[17] an exercise of no trifling fatigue, or resolution; for among the things to be gained by seeing the lakes is a conception of the extreme wildness of their boundaries. You arrive with a notion, that you can and dare rove any where amongst the mountains; and have only to see three to have the utmost terror of losing your way.

The danger of wandering in these regions without a guide is increased by an uncertainty, as to the titles of heights; for the people of each village have a name for the part of a mountain nearest to themselves, and they sometimes call the whole by that name. The circumference of such heights is also too vast, and the flexures too numerous to admit of great accuracy. Skiddaw, Saddleback and Helvellyn, may however, be certainly distinguished. There are others, a passage over which would save, perhaps, eight or ten miles out of twenty, but which are so little known, except to the shepherds, that they are very rarely crossed by travellers. We could not trust to any person's knowledge of Harter-fell, beyond the head of Haweswater.

HAWESWATER

THIS IS A LAKE, of which little has been mentioned, perhaps because it is inferiour in size to the others, but which is distinguished by the solemn grandeur of its rocks and mountains, that rise in very bold and awful characters. The water, about three miles long, and at the widest only half a mile over, nearly describes the figure 8, being narrowed in the centre by the projecting shores; and, at this spot, it is said to be fifty fathom deep.

Crossing the meadows of Bampton vale and ascending the opposite heights, we approached the fells of Haweswater, and, having proceeded for a mile along the side of hills, the views over the vale and of the southern mountains changing with almost every step, the lake began to open between a very lofty ridge, covered with forest, and abrupt fells of heath, or naked rock. Soon after, we looked upon the first expanse of the lake. Its eastern shore, rising in a tremendous ridge of rocks, darkened with wood to the summit, appears to terminate in Wallow-crag, a promontory of towering height, beyond which the lake winds from view. The finely broken mountains on the west are covered with heath, and the tops impend in crags and precipices; but their ascent from the water is less sudden than that of the opposite rocks, and they are skirted by a narrow margin of vivid green, where cattle were feeding, and tufted shrubs and little groves overhung the lake and were reflected on its dark surface. Above, a very few white cottages among wood broke in upon the solitude; higher still, the mountain-flocks were browsing, and above all, the narrow perspective was closed by dark and monstrous summits.

As we wound along the bank, the rocks unfolded and disclosed the second expanse, with scenery yet more towering and sublime than the first. This perspective seemed to be terminated by the huge mountain called Castle-street; but, as we advanced, Harter-fell reared his awful front, impending over the water, and shut in the scene, where, amidst rocks, and at the entrance of a glen almost choked by fragments from the heights, stands the chapel of Martindale, spoken by the country people Mardale. Among the fells of this dark prospect are Lathale, Winter-crag, Castle crag and Riggindale, their bold lines appearing beyond each other as they fell into the upper part of the lake, and some of them shewing only masses of shattered rock. Kidstow-pike is pre-eminent among the crowding summits beyond the eastern shore, and the clouds frequently spread their gloom over its point, or fall in showers into the cup within; on the west High-street, which overlooks the head of Ullswater, is the most dignified of the mountains.

Leaving the green margin of the lake, we ascended to the Parsonage, a low, white building on a knoll, sheltered by the mountain and a grove of sycamores, with a small garden in front, falling towards the water.[18] From the door we had a view of the whole lake and the surrounding fells, which the eminence we were upon was just raised enough to shew to advantage. Nearly opposite to it the bold promontory of Wallow-crag pushed its base into the lake, where a peninsula advanced to meet it, spread with bright verdure, on which the hamlet of Martindale lay half concealed among a grove of oak, beech and sycamore, whose tints contrasted with the darker one of the spiry spruce, or more clumped English sir, and accorded sweetly with the pastoral green beneath. The ridge of precipices, that swept from Wallow-crag southward, and formed a bay for the upper part of the lake, was despoiled of its forest; but that, which curved northward, was dark with dwarf-wood to the water's brim, and, opening distantly to Bampton vale, let in a gay miniature landscape, bright in sunshine. Below, the lake reflected the gloom of the woods, and was sometimes marked with long white lines, which, we were told, indicated bad weather; but, except when a sudden gust swept the surface, it gave back every image on the shore, as in a dark mirror.

The interior of the Parsonage was as comfortable as the situation was interesting. A neat parlour opened from the passage, but it was newly painted, and we were shewn into the family room, having a large old-fashioned chimney corner, with benches to receive a social party, and forming a most enviable retreat from the storms of the mountains. Here, in the winter evening, a family circle, gathering round a blazing pile of wood on the hearth, might defy the weather and the world. It was delightful to picture such a party, happy in their home, in the sweet affections of kindred and in honest independence, conversing, working and reading occasionally, while the blast was struggling against the casement and the snow pelting on the roof.

The seat of a long window, overlooking the lake, offered the delights of other seasons; hence the luxuriance of summer and the colouring of autumn successively spread their enchantments over the opposite woods, and the meadows that margined the water below; and a little garden of sweets sent up its fragrance to that of the honeysuckles, that twined round the window. Here, too, lay a store of books, and, to instance that an inhabitant of this remote nook could not exclude an interest concerning the distant world, among them was a history of passing events. Alas! to what scenes, to what display of human passions and human suffering did it open! How opposite to the simplicity, the innocence and the peace of these!

The venerable father of the mansion was engaged in his duty at his chapel of Martindale, but we were hospitably received within, and heard the next day how gladly he would have rendered any civilities to strangers.[19]

On leaving this enviable little residence, we pursued the steeps of the mountain behind it, and were soon amidst the flocks and the crags, whence the look-down upon the lake and among the fells was solemn and surprising. About a quarter of a mile from the Parsonage, a torrent of some dignity rushed past us, foaming down a rocky chasm in its way to the lake. Every where, little streams of chrystal clearness wandered silently among the moss and turf, which half concealed their progress, or dashed over the rocks; and, across the largest, sheep-bridges of flat stone were thrown, to prevent the flocks from being carried away in attempting to pass them in winter. The grey stones, that grew among the heath, were spotted with mosses of so fine a texture, that it was difficult to ascertain whether they were vegetable; their tints were a delicate pea-green and primrose, with a variety of colours, which it was not necessary to be a botanist to admire.[20]

An hour, passed in ascending, brought us to the brow of Bampton vale, which sloped gently downward to the north, where it opened to lines of distant mountains, that extended far into the east. The woods of Lowther-park capped two remote hills, and spread luxuriantly down their sides into the valley; and nearer, Bampton grange lay at the base of a mountain, crowned with fir plantations, over which, in a distant vale, we discovered the village of Shap and long ridges of the highland, passed on the preceding day.

One of the fells we had just crossed is called Blanarasa, at the summit of which two grey stones, each about four feet high, and placed upright, at the distance of nine feet from each other, remain of four, which are remembered to have been formerly there. The place is still called Four Stones; but tradition does not relate the design of the monument; whether to limit adjoining districts, or to commemorate a battle, or a hero.

We descended gradually into the vale, among thickets of rough oaks, on the bank of a rivulet, which foamed in a deep channel beneath their foliage, and came to a glade so sequestered and gloomily overshadowed, that one almost expected to see the venerable arch of a ruin, peeping between the branches. It was the very spot, which the founder of a monastery might have chosen for his retirement, where the chantings of a choir might have mingled with the soothing murmur of the stream, and monks have glided beneath the solemn trees in garments scarcely distinguishable from the shades themselves.

This glade, sloping from the eye, opened under spreading oaks to a remote glimpse of the vale, with blue hills in the distance; and on the grassy hillocks of the fore-ground cattle were every where reposing.

We returned, about sunset, to Bampton, after a walk of little more than four miles, which had exhibited a great variety of scenery, beautiful, romantic and sublime. At the entrance of the village, the Lowther and a nameless rivulet, that runs from Haweswater, join their waters; both streams were now sunk in their beds; but in winter they sometimes contend for the conquest and ravage of the neighbouring plains. The waters have then risen to the height of five or six feet in a meadow forty yards from their summer channels. In an inclosure of this vale was fought the last battle, or skirmish, with the Scots in Westmoreland; and it is within the telling of the sons of great-grandfathers, that the contest continued, till the Scots were discovered to fire only pebbles; the villagers had then the folly to close with them and the success to drive them away; but such was the simplicity of the times, that it was called a victory to have made one prisoner. Stories of this sort are not yet entirely forgotten in the deeply inclosed vales of Westmoreland and Cumberland, where the greater part of the present inhabitants can refer to an ancestry of several centuries, on the same spot.

We thought Bampton, though a very ill-built village, an enviable spot; having a clergyman, as we heard, of exemplary manners, and, as one of us witnessed, of a most faithful earnestness in addressing his congregation in the church; being but slightly removed from one of the lakes, that accumulates in a small space many of the varieties and attractions of the others; and having the adjoining lands distributed, for the most part, into small farms, so that, as it is not thought low to be without wealth, the poor do not acquire the offensive and disreputable habits, by which they are too often tempted to revenge, or resist the ostentation of the rich.

ULLSWATER

THE RIDE from Bampton to Ullswater is very various and delightful. It winds for about three miles along the western heights of this green and open vale, among embowered lanes, that alternately admit and exclude the pastoral scenes below, and the fine landscapes on the opposite hills, formed by the plantations and antient woods of Lowther-park. These spread over a long tract, and mingle in sweet variety with the lively verdure of lawns and meadows, that slope into the valley, and sometimes appear in gleams among the dark thickets. The house, of white stone with red window-cases, embosomed among the woods, has nothing in its appearance answerable to the surrounding grounds. Its situation and that of the park are exquisitely happy, just where the vale of Bampton opens to that of Eden, and the long mountainous ridge and peak of Cross-fell, aspiring above them all, stretch before the eye; with the town of Penrith shelving along the side of a distant mountain, and its beacon on the summit; the ruins of its castle appearing distinctly at the same time, crowning a low round hill. The horizon to the north and the east is bounded by lines of mountains, range above range, not romantic and surprising, but multitudinous and vast. Of these, Cross-fell, said to be the highest mountain in Cumberland, gives its name to the whole northern ridge, which in its full extent, from the neighbourhood of Gillsland to that of Kirkby-Steven, is near fifty miles. This perspective of the extensive vale of Eden has grandeur and magnificence in as high a degree as that of Bampton has pastoral beauty, closing in the gloomy solitudes of Haweswater. The vale is finely wooded, and variegated with mansions, parks, meadow-land, corn, towns, villages, and all that make a distant landscape rich. Among the peculiarities of it, are little mountains of alpine shape, that start up like pyramids in the middle of the vale, some covered with wood, others barren and rocky. The scene perhaps only wants a river like the Rhine, or the Thames, to make it the very finest in England for union of grandeur, beauty and extent.

Opposite Lowther-hall, we gave a farewell look to the pleasant vale of Bampton and its southern fells, as the road, winding more to the west, led us over the high lands, that separate it from the vale of Emont. Then, ascending through shady lanes and among fields where the oat harvest was gathering, we had enchanting retrospects of the vale of Eden, spreading to the east, with all its chain of mountains chequered by the autumnal shadows.

Soon after, the road brought us to the brows of Emont, a narrow well-wooded vale, the river, from which it takes its name, meandering through it from Ullswater among pastures and pleasure-grounds, to meet the Lowther near Brougham Castle. Penrith and its castle and beacon look up the vale from the north, and the astonishing fells of Ullswater close upon it in the south; while Delemain, the house and beautiful grounds of Mr. Hassel, Hutton St. John, a venerable mansion, and the single tower called Dacre-castle adorn the valley.[21] But who can pause to admire the elegancies of art, when surrounded by the wonders of nature? The approach to this sublime lake along the heights of Emont is exquisitely interesting; for the road, being shrouded by woods, allows the eye only partial glimpses of the gigantic shapes, that are assembled in the distance, and, awakening high expectation, leaves the imagination, thus elevated, to paint the 'forms of things unseen.'[22] Thus it was, when we caught a first view of the dark broken tops of the fells, that rise round Ullswater, of size and shape most huge, bold, and awful; overspread with a blue mysterious tint, that seemed almost supernatural, though according in gloom and sublimity with the severe features it involved.

Further on, the mountains began to unfold themselves; their outlines, broken, abrupt and intersecting each other in innumerable directions, seemed, now and then, to fall back like a multitude at some supreme command, and permitted an oblique glimpse into the deep vales. A close lane then descended towards Pooly-bridge, where, at length, the lake itself appeared beyond the spreading branches, and, soon after, the first reach expanded before us, with all its mountains tumbled round it; rocky, ruinous and vast, impending, yet rising in wild confusion and multiplied points behind each other.

This view of the first reach from the foot of Dunmallet, a pointed woody hill, near Pooly-bridge, is one of the finest on the lake, which here spreads in a noble sheet, near three miles long, and almost two miles broad, to the base of Thwaithill-nab, winding round which it disappears, and the whole is then believed to be seen. The character of this view is nearly that of simple grandeur; the mountains, that impend over the shore in front, are peculiarly awful in their forms and attitudes; on the left, the fells soften; woodlands, and their pastures, colour their lower declivities, and the water is margined with the tenderest verdure, opposed to the dark woods and crags above. On the right, a green conical hill slopes to the shore, where cattle were reposing on the grass, or sipping the clear wave; further, rise the bolder rocks of Thwaithill-nab, where the lake disappears, and, beyond, the dark precipices and summits of fells, that crown the second reach.

Winding the foot of Dunmallet, the almost pyramidal hill, that shuts up this end of Ullswater, and separates it from the vale of Emont, we crossed Barton bridge, where this little river, clear as crystal, issues from the lake, and through a close pass hurries over a rocky channel to the vale. Its woody steeps, the tufted island, that interrupts its stream, and the valley beyond, form altogether a picture in fine contrast with the majesty of Ullswater, expanding on the other side of the bridge.

We followed the skirts of a smooth green hill, the lake, on the other hand, flowing softly against the road and shewing every pebble on the beach beneath, and proceeded towards the second bend; but soon mounted from the shore among the broken knolls of Dacre-common, whence we had various views of the first reach, its scenery appearing in darkened majesty as the autumnal shadows swept over it. Sometimes, however, the rays, falling in gleams upon the water, gave it the finest silvery tone imaginable, sober though splendid. Dunmallet at the foot of the lake was a formal unpleasing object, not large enough to be grand, or wild enough to be romantic.

The ground of the common is finely broken, and is scattered sparingly with white cottages, each picturesquely shadowed by its dark grove; above, rise plantations and gray crags which lead the eye forward to the alpine forms, that crown the second reach, changing their attitudes every instant as they are approached.

Ullswater in all its windings, which give it the form of the letter S, is nearly nine miles long; the width is various, sometimes nearly two miles and seldom less than one; but Skelling-nab, a vast rock in the second reach, projects so as to reduce it to less than a quarter of a mile. These are chiefly the reputed measurements, but the eye loses its power of judging even of the breadth, confounded by the boldness of the shores and the grandeur of the fells, that rise beyond; the proportions however are grand, for the water retains its dignity, notwithstanding the vastness of its accompaniments; a circumstance, which Derwentwater can scarcely boast.

The second bend, assuming the form of a river, is very long, but generally broad, and brought strongly to remembrance some of the passes of the Rhine beyond Coblentz: though, here, the rocks, that rise over the water, are little wooded; and, there, their skirts are never margined by pasture, or open to such fairy summer scenes of vivid green mingling with shades of wood and gleams of corn, as sometimes appear within the recesses of these wintry mountains. These cliffs, however, do not shew the variety of hue, or marbled veins, that frequently surprise and delight on the Rhine, being generally dark and gray, and the varieties in their complexion, when there are any, purely aerial; but they are vast and broken; rise immediately from the stream, and often shoot their masses over it; while the expanse of water below accords with the dignity of that river in many of its reaches. Once too, there were other points of resemblance, in the ruins of monasteries and convents, which, though reason rejoices that they no longer exist, the eye may be allowed to regret. Of these, all which now remains on record is, that a society of Benedictine monks was founded on the summit of Dunmallet, and a nunnery of the same order on a point behind Sowlby-fell; traces of these ruins, it is said, may still be seen.[23]

Thus grandeur and immensity are the characteristics of the left shore of the second reach; the right exhibits romantic wildness in the rough ground of Dacre-common and the craggy heights above, and, further on, the sweetest forms of reposing beauty, in the grassy hillocks and undulating copses of Gowbarrow-park, fringing the water, sometimes over little rocky eminences, that project into the stream, and, at others, in shelving bays, where the lake, transparent as crystal, breaks upon the pebbly bank, and laves the road, that winds there. Above these pastoral and sylvan landscapes, rise broken precipices, less tremendous than those of the opposite shore, with pastures pursuing the crags to a considerable height, speckled with cattle, which are exquisitely picturesque, as they graze upon the knolls and among the old trees, that adorn this finely declining park.

Leaving the hamlet of Watermillock at some distance on the left, and passing the seat of Mr. Robinson, sequestered in the gloom of beech and sycamores, there are fine views over the second reach, as the road descends the common towards Gowbarrow.[24] Among the boldest fells, that breast the lake on the left shore, are Holling-fell and Swarth-fell, now no longer boasting any part of the forest of Martindale, but shewing huge walls of naked rock, and scars, which many torrents have inflicted. One channel only in this dry season retained its shining stream; the chasm was dreadful, parting the mountain from the summit to the base; and its waters in winter, leaping in foam from precipice to precipice, must be infinitely sublime; not, however, even then from their mass, but from the length and precipitancy of their descent.

The perspective as the road descends into Gowbarrow-park is perhaps the very finest on the lake. The scenery of the first reach is almost tame when compared with this, and it is difficult to say where it can be equalled for Alpine sublimity, and for effecting wonder and awful elevation. The lake, after expanding at a distance to great breadth, once more loses itself beyond the enormous pile of rock called Place-fell, opposite to which the shore, seeming to close upon all further progress, is bounded by two promontories covered with woods, that shoot their luxuriant foliage to the water's edge. The shattered mass of gray rock, called Yew-crag, rises immediately over these, and, beyond, a glen opens to a chaos of mountains more solemn in their aspect, and singular in their shapes, than any which have appeared, point crowding over point in lofty succession. Among these is Stone-cross-pike and huge Helvellyn, scowling over all; but, though this retains its pre eminence, its dignity is lost in the mass of alps around and below it. A fearful gloom involved them; the shadows of a stormy sky upon mountains of dark rock and heath. All this is seen over the woody fore-ground of the park, which, soon shrouding us in its bowery lanes, allowed the eye and the fancy to repose, while venturing towards new forms and assemblages of sublimity.

Meantime, the green shade, under which we passed, where the sultry low of cattle, and the sound of streams hurrying from the heights through the copses of Gowbarrow to the lake below, were all that broke the stillness; these, with gleamings of the water, close on the left, between the foliage, and which was ever changing its hue, sometimes assuming the soft purple of a pigeon's neck, at others the silvery tint of sunshine—these circumstances of imagery were in soothing and beautiful variety with the gigantic visions we had lost.

The road still pursuing this border of the lake, the copses opened to partial views of the bold rocks, that form the opposite shore, and many a wild recess and solemn glen appeared and vanished among them, some shewing only broken fells, the sides of others shaggy with forests, and nearly all lined, at their bases, with narrow pastures of the most exquisite verdure. Thus descending upon a succession of sweeping bays, where the shades parted, and admitted the lake, that flowed even with us, and again retreating from it over gentle eminences, where it glittered only between the leaves; crossing the rude bridges of several becks, rapid, clear and foaming among dark stones, and receiving a green tint from the closely shadowing trees, but neither precipitous enough in their descent, nor ample enough in their course, to increase the dignity of the scene, we came, after passing nearly three miles through the park, to Lyulph's Tower. This mansion, a square, gray edifice, with turreted corners, battlements and windows in the Gothic style, has been built by the present Duke of Norfolk in one of the finest situations of a park, abounding with views of the grand and the sublime. It stands on a green eminence, a little removed from the water, backed with wood and with pastures rising abruptly beyond, to the cliffs and crags that crown them.[25] In front, the ground falls finely to the lake's edge, broken, yet gentle, and scattered over with old trees, and darkened with copses, which mingle in fine variety of tints with the light verdure of the turf beneath. Herds of deer, wandering over the knolls, and cattle, reposing in the shade, completed this sweet landscape.

The lake is hence seen to make one of its boldest expanses, as it sweeps round Place-fell, and flows into the third and last bend of this wonderful vale. Lyulph's Tower looks up this reach to the south, and to the east traces all the fells and curving banks of Gowbarrow, that bind the second; while, to the west, a dark glen opens to a glimpse of the solemn alps round Helvellyn; and all these objects are seen over the mild beauty of the park.

Passing fine sweeps of the shore and over bold headlands, we came opposite to the vast promontory, called Place-fell, that pushes its craggy foot into the lake, like a lion's claw, round which the waters make a sudden turn, and enter Patterdale, their third and final expanse. In this reach, they lose the form of a river, and resume that of a lake, being closed, at three miles distance, by the ruinous rocks, that guard the gorge of Patterdale, backed by a multitude of fells. The water, in this scope, is of oval form, bounded on one side by the precipices of Place-fell, Martindale-fell, and several others equally rude and awful that rise from its edge, and shew no lines of verdure, or masses of wood, but retire in rocky bays, or project in vast promontories athwart it. The opposite shore is less severe and more romantic; the rocks are lower and richly wooded, and, often receding from the water, leave room for a tract of pasture, meadow land and corn, to margin their ruggedness. At the upper end, the village of Patterdale, and one or two white farms, peep out from among trees beneath the scowling mountains, that close the scene; pitched in a rocky nook, with corn and meadow land, sloping gently in front to the lake, and, here and there, a scattered grove. But this scene is viewed to more advantage from one of the two woody eminences, that overhang the lake, just at the point where it forms its last angle, and, like an opened compass, spreads its two arms before the eye. These heights are extremely beautiful, viewed from the opposite shore, and had long charmed us at a distance. Approaching them, we crossed another torrent, Glencoyn-beck, or Airey-force, which here divides not only the estates of the Duke of Norfolk and Mr. Hodgkinson, but the counties of Westmoreland and Cumberland; and all the fells beyond, that enclose the last bend of Ullswater, are in Patterdale. Here, on the right, at the feet of awful rocks, was spread a gay autumnal scene, in which the peasants were singing merrily as they gathered the oats into sheafs; woods, turfy hillocks, and, above all, tremendous crags, abruptly closing round the yellow harvest. The figures, together with the whole landscape, resembled one of those beautifully fantastic scenes, which fable calls up before the wand of the magician.

Entering Glencoyn woods and sweeping the boldest bay of the lake, while the water dashed with a strong surge upon the shore, we at length mounted a road frightful from its steepness and its crags, and gained one of the wooded summits so long admired. From hence the view of Ullswater is the most extensive and various, that its shores exhibit, comprehending its two principal reaches, and though not the most picturesque, it is certainly the most grand. To the east, extends the middle sweep in long and equal perspective, walled with barren fells on the right, and margined on the left with the pastoral recesses and bowery projections of Gowbarrow park. The rude mountains above almost seemed to have fallen back from the shore to admit this landscape within their hollow bosom, and then, bending abruptly, appear, like Milton's Adam viewing the sleeping Eve, to hang over it enamoured.

Lyulph's Tower is the only object of art, except the hamlet of Watermillock, seen in the distant perspective, that appears in the second bend of Ullswater; and this loses much of its effect from the square uniformity of the structure, and the glaring green of its painted window-cases. This is the longest reach of the lake.

Place-fell, which divides the two last bends, and was immediately opposite to the point we were on, is of the boldest form. It projects into the water, an enormous mass of grey crag, scarred with dark hues; thence retiring a little it again bends forward in huge cliffs, and finally starts up into a vast perpendicular face of rock. As a single object, it is wonderfully grand; and, connected with the scene, its effect is sublime. The lower rocks are called Silver-rays, and not inaptly; for, when the sun shines upon them, their variegated sides somewhat resemble in brightness the rays streaming beneath a cloud.

The last reach of Ullswater, which is on the right of this point, expands into an oval, and its majestic surface is spotted with little rocky islets, that would adorn a less sacred scene; here they are prettinesses, that can scarcely be tolerated by the grandeur of its character. The tremendous mountains, which scowl over the gorge of Patterdale; the cliffs, massy, broken and overlooked by a multitude of dark summits, with the grey walls of Swarth and Martindale fells, that upheave themselves on the eastern shore, form altogether one of the most grand and awful pictures on the lake; yet, admirable and impressive as it is, as to solemnity and astonishment, its effect with us was not equal to that of the more alpine sketch, caught in distant perspective from the descent into Gowbarrow-park.

In these views of Ullswater, sublimity and greatness are the predominating characters, though beauty often glows upon the western bank. The mountains are all bold, gloomy and severe. When we saw them, the sky accorded well with the scene, being frequently darkened by autumnal clouds; and the equinoctial gale swept the surface of the lake, marking its blackness with long white lines, and beating its waves over the rocks to the foliage of the thickets above. The trees, that shade these eminences, give greater force to the scenes, which they either partially exclude, or wholly admit, and become themselves fine objects, enriched as they are with the darkest moss.

From hence the ride to the village of Patterdale, at the lake's head, is, for the first part, over precipices covered with wood, whence you look down, on the left, upon the water, or upon pastures stretching to it; on the right, the rocks rise abruptly, and often impend their masses over the road; or open to narrow dells, green, rocky and overlooked by endless mountains.

About half way to the village of Patterdale, a peninsula spreads from this shore into the lake, where a white house, peeping from a grove and surrounded with green enclosures, is beautifully placed. This is an inn, and, perhaps, the principal one, as to accommodation; but, though its situation, on a spot which on each side commands the lake, is very fine, it is not comparable, in point of wildness and sublimity, to that of the cottage, called the King's Arms, at Patterdale. In the way thither, are enchanting catches of the lake, between the trees on the left, and peeps into the glens, that wind among the alps towards Helvellyn, on the right. These multiply near the head of Ullswater, where they start off as from one point, like radii, and conclude in trackless solitudes.

It is difficult to spread varied pictures of such scenes before the imagination. A repetition of the same images of rock, wood and water, and the same epithets of grand, vast and sublime, which necessarily occur, must appear tautologous, on paper, though their archetypes in nature, ever varying in outline, or arrangement, exhibit new visions to the eye, and produce new shades of effect on the mind. It is difficult also, where these delightful differences have been experienced, to forbear dwelling on the remembrance, and attempting to sketch the peculiarities, which occasioned them. The scenery at the head of Ullswater is especially productive of such difficulties, where a wish to present the picture, and a consciousness of the impossibility of doing so, except by the pencil, meet and oppose each other.

Patterdale itself is a name somewhat familiar to recollection, from the circumstance of the chief estate in it having given to its possessors, for several centuries, the title of Kings of Patterdale. The last person so distinguished was richer than his ancestors, having increased his income, by the most ludicrous parsimony, to a thousand pounds a year. His son and successor is an industrious country gentleman, who has improved the sort of farming mansion, annexed to the estate, and, not affecting to depart much from the simple manners of the other inhabitants, is respectable enough to be generally called by his own name of Mounsey, instead of the title, which was probably seldom given to his ancestors, but in some sort of mockery.[26]

Engraving of Patterdale Palace, pub. Sherwood, Jones and Co, c.1827

The village is very humble, as to the conditions and views of the inhabitants; and very respectable, as to their integrity and simplicity, and to the contentment, which is proved by the infrequency of emigrations to other districts. It straggles at the feet of fells, somewhat removed from the lake and near the entrance of the wild vale of Glenridding. Its white church is seen nearly from the commencement of the last reach, rising among trees, and in the church-yard are the ruins of an antient yew, of remarkable size and venerable beauty; its trunk, hollowed and silvered by age, resembles twisted roots; yet the branches, that remain above, are not of melancholy black, but flourish in rich verdure and flaky foliage.

The inn is beyond the village, securely sheltered under high crags, while enormous fells, close on the right, open to the gorge of Patterdale; and Goldrill-beck, issuing from it, descends among the corn and meadows, to join the lake at a little distance. We had a happy evening at this cleanly cottage, where there was no want, without its recompense, from the civil offices of the people. Among the rocks, that rose over it, is a station, which has been more frequently selected than any other on the lake by the painter and the lover of the *beau idée*, as the French and Sir Joshua Reynolds expressively term what Mr. Burke explains in his definition of the word *fine*.[27] Below the point, on which we stood, a tract of corn and meadow land fell gently to the lake, which expanded in great majesty beyond, bounded on the right by the precipices of many fells, and, on the left, by rocks finely wooded, and of more broken and spiry outline. The undulating pastures and copses of Gowbarrow closed the perspective. Round the whole of these shores, but particularly on the left, rose clusters of dark and pointed summits, assuming great variety of shape, amongst which Helvellyn was still pre-eminent. Immediately around us, all was vast and gloomy; the fells mount swiftly and to enormous heights, leaving at their bases only crags and hillock, tufted with thickets of dwarf-oak and holly, where the beautiful cattle, that adorned them, and a few sheep, were picking a scanty supper among the heath.

From this spot glens open on either hand, that lead the eye only to a chaos of mountains. The profile of one near the sore-ground on the right is remarkably grand, shelving from the summit in one vast sweep of rock, with only some interruption of craggy points near its base, into the water. On one side, it unites with the fells in the gorge of Patterdale, and, on the other, winds into a bold bay for the lake. Among the highlands, seen over the left shore, is Common-fell, a large heathy mountain, which appeared to face us. Somewhat nearer, is a lower one, called Glenridding, and above it the Nab. Grassdale has Glenridding and the Nab on one side towards the water, and Birks-fell and St. Sunday's-crag over that, on the other. The points, that rise above the Nab, are Stridon-edge, then Cove's head, and, over all, the precipices of dark Helvellyn, now appearing only at intervals among the clouds.

Not only every fell of this wild region has a name, but almost every crag of every fell, so that shepherds sitting at the fire-side can direct each other to the exact spot among the mountains, where a stray sheep has been seen.

Among the rocks on the right shore, is Martindale-fell, once shaded with a forest, from which it received its name, and which spreading to a vast extent over the hills and vallies beyond, even as far as Haweswater, darkened the front of Swarth-fell and several others, that impend over the first and second reach of Ullswater. Of the mountains, which tower above the glen of Patterdale, the highest are Harter's-fell, Kidstow-pike, and the ridge, called the High-street; a name, which reminded us of the German denomination, *Berg strasse*.[28]

The effect of a stormy evening upon the scenery was solemn. Clouds smoked along the fells, veiling them for a moment, and passing on to other summits; or sometimes they involved the lower steeps, leaving the tops unobscured and resembling islands in a distant ocean. The lake was dark and tempestuous, dashing the rocks with a strong foam. It was a scene worthy of the sublimity of Ossian, and brought to recollection some touches of his gloomy pencil. 'When the storms of the mountains come, when the north lifts the waves on high, I sit by the sounding shore, &c.'[29]

A large hawk, sailing proudly in the air, and wheeling among the stormy clouds, superior to the shock of the gust, was the only animated object in the upward prospect. We were told, that the eagles had forsaken their aeries in this neighbourhood and in Borrowdale, and are fled to the Isle of Man; but one had been seen in Patterdale, the day before, which, not being at its full growth, could not have arrived from a great distance.

We returned to our low-roofed habitation, where, as the wind swept in hollow gusts along the mountains and strove against our casements, the crackling blaze of a wood fire lighted up the cheerfulness, which, so long since as Juvenal's time, has been allowed to arise from the contrast of ease against difficulty.[30] *Suave mari magno, turbantibus aequora ventis*;[31] and, however we might exclaim,

———————————'be my retreat
Between the groaning forest and the shore,
Beat by the boundless multitude of waves!'

it was pleasant to add,

'Where ruddy fire and beaming tapers join
To cheer the gloom.'[32]

BROUGHAM CASTLE

THE NEXT MORNING, we proceeded from Ullswater along the vale of Emont, so sweetly adorned by the woods and lawns of Dalemain, the seat of Mr. Hassel, whose mansion is seen in the bottom. One of the most magnificent prospects in the country is when this vale opens to that of Eden. The mountainous range of Cross-fell fronted us, and its appearance, this day, was very striking, for the effect of autumnal light and shade. The upper range, bright in sunshine, appeared to rise, like light clouds above the lower, which was involved in dark shadow, so that it was a considerable time before the eye could detect the illusion. The effect of this was inexpressibly interesting.

Within view of Emont bridge, which divides the counties of Cumberland and Westmoreland, is that memorial of antient times, so often described under the name of Arthur's Round Table; a green circular spot of forty paces diameter, inclosed by a dry ditch, and, beyond this, by a bank; each in sufficient preservation to shew exactly what has been its form. In the midst of the larger circle is another of only seven paces diameter. We have no means of adding to, or even of corroborating any of the well known conjectures, concerning the use of this rude and certainly very antient monument. Those not qualified to propose decisions in this respect may, however, suffer themselves to believe, that the bank without the ditch and the enclosure within it were places for different classes of persons, interested as parties, or spectators, in some transactions, passing within the inner circle; and that these, whether religious, civil, or military ceremonies, were rendered distinct and conspicuous, for the purpose of impressing them upon the memory of the spectators, at a time when memory and tradition were the only preservatives of history.

Passing a bridge, under which the Lowther, from winding and romantic banks, enters the vale of Eden, we ascended between the groves of Bird's Nest, or, as it is now called, Brougham Hall; a white mansion, with battlements and gothic windows, having formerly a bird painted on the front. It is perched among woods, on the brow of a steep, but not lofty hill, and commands enchanting prospects over the vale. The winding Emont; the ruins of Brougham Castle on a green knoll of Whinfield park, surrounded with old groves; far beyond this, the highlands of Cross-fell; to the north, Carleton-hall, the handsome modern mansion of Mr. Wallace, amidst lawns of incomparable verdure and luxuriant woods falling from the heights;[33] further still, the mountain, town and beacon of Penrith; these are the principal features of the rich landscape, spread before the eye from the summit of the hill, at Bird's Nest.

As we descended to Brougham Castle, about a mile further, its ruined masses of pale red stone, tufted with shrubs and plants, appeared between groves of fir, beach, oak and ash, amidst the broken ground of Whinfield park, a quarter of a mile through which brought us to the ruin itself. It was guarded by a sturdy mastiff, worthy the office of porter to such a place, and a good effigy of the Sir Porter of a former age. Brougham Castle, venerable for its well certified antiquity and for the hoary masses it now exhibits, is rendered more interesting by having been occasionally the residence of the humane and generous Sir Philip Sydney; who had only to look from the windows of this once noble edifice to see his own 'Arcadia' spreading on every side. The landscape probably awakened his imagination, for it was during a visit here, that the greatest part of that work was written.[34]

Engraving of Brougham Castle by Godfrey, 1774

This edifice, once amongst the strongest and most important of the border fortresses, is supposed to have been founded by the Romans;[35] but the first historical record concerning it is dated in the time of William the Conqueror, who granted it to his nephew, Hugh de Albinois. His successors held it, till 1170, when Hugh de Morville, one of the murderers of Thomas a Becket, forfeited it by his crime. Brougham was afterwards granted by King John to a grandson of Hugh, Robert de Vipont, whose grandson again forfeited the estate, which was, however, restored to his daughters, one of whom marrying a De Clifford, it remained in this family, till a daughter of the celebrated Countess of Pembroke gave it by marriage to that of the Tuftons, Earls of Thanet, in which it now remains.[36]

This castle has been thrice nearly demolished; first by neglect, during the minority of Roger de Vipont, after which it was sufficiently restored to receive James the First, on his return from Scotland, in 1617; secondly, in the civil wars of Charles the First's time; and thirdly, in 1728, when great part of the edifice was deliberately taken down, and the materials sold for one hundred pounds. Some of the walls still remaining are twelve feet thick, and the places are visible, in which the massy gates were held to them by hinges and bolts of uncommon size. A fuller proof of the many sacrifices of comfort and convenience, by which the highest classes in former ages were glad to purchase security, is very seldom afforded, than by the three detached parts still left of this edifice; but they shew nothing of the magnificence and gracefulness, which so often charm the eye in gothic ruins. Instead of these, they exhibit symptoms of the cruelties, by which their first lords revenged upon others the wretchedness of the continual suspicion felt by themselves. Dungeons, secret passages and heavy iron rings remain to hint of unhappy wretches, who were, perhaps, rescued only by death from these horrible engines of a tyrant's will. The bones probably of such victims are laid beneath the damp earth of these vaults.

A young woman from a neighbouring farm-house conducted us over broken banks, washed by the Emont, to what had been the grand entrance of the castle; a venerable gothic gateway, dark and of great depth, passing under a square tower, finely shadowed by old elms. Above, are a cross-loop and two tier of small pointed windows; no battlements appear at the top; but four rows of corbels, which probably once supported them, now prop some tufts of antient thorn, that have roots in their fractures.

As we passed under this long gateway, we looked into what is still called the Keep, a small vaulted room, receiving light only from loops in the outward wall. Near a large fire-place, yet entire, is a trap door leading to the dungeon below; and, in an opposite corner, a door-case to narrow stairs, that wind up the turret, where too, as well as in the vault, prisoners were probably secured. One almost saw the surly keeper descending through this door-case, and heard him rattle the keys of the chambers above, listening with indifference to the clank of chains and to the echo of that groan below, which seemed to rend the heart it burst from.

This gloomy gateway, which had once sounded with the trumpets and horses of James the First, when he visited the Earl of Cumberland, this gateway, now serving only to shelter cattle from the storm, opens, at length, to a grassy knoll, with bold masses of the ruin scattered round it and a few old ash trees, waving in the area. Through a fractured arch in the rampart some features in the scenery without appear to advantage; the Emont falling over a weir at some distance, with fulling-mills on the bank above;[37] beyond, the pastured slopes and woodlands of Carleton park, and Cross-fell sweeping the back-ground.

Of the three ruinous parts, that now remain of the edifice, one large square mass, near the tower and gateway, appears to have contained the principal apartments; the walls are of great height, and, though roofless, nearly entire. We entered what seemed to have been the great hall, now choaked with rubbish and weeds. It was interesting to look upwards through the void, and trace by the many window-cases, that appeared at different heights in the walls, somewhat of the plan of apartments, whose floors and ceilings had long since vanished; majestic reliques, which shewed, that here, as well as at Hardwick, the chief rooms had been in the second story.[38] Door-cases, that had opened to rooms without this building, with remains of passages within the walls, were frequently seen, and, here and there, in a corner at a vast height, fragments of a winding staircase, appearing beyond the arch of a slender door-way.

We were tempted to enter a ruinous passage below, formed in the great thickness of the walls; but it was soon lost in darkness, and we were told that no person had ventured to explore the end of this, or of many similar passages among the ruins, now the dens of serpents and other venomous reptiles. It was probably a secret way to the great dungeon, which may still be seen, underneath the hall; for the roof remains, though what was called the Sweating Pillar, from the dew, that was owing to its damp situation and its seclusion from outward air, no longer supports it. Large iron rings, fastened to the carved heads of animals, are still shewn in the walls of this dungeon. Not a single loop-hole was left by the contriver of this hideous vault for the refreshment of prisoners; yet were they insulted by some display of gothic elegance, for the pillar already mentioned, supporting the centre of the roof, spread from thence into eight branches, which descended the walls, and terminated at the floor in the heads, holding the iron rings.

The second mass of the ruin, which, though at a considerable distance from the main building, was formerly connected with it, shews the walls of many small chambers, with reliques of the passages and stairs, that led to them. But, perhaps, the only picturesque feature of the castle is the third detachment; a small tower finely shattered, having near its top a flourishing ash, growing from the solid walls, and overlooking what was once the moat. We mounted a perilous stair-case, of which many steps were gone, and others trembled to the pressure; then gained a turret, of which two sides were also fallen, and, at length, ascended to the whole magnificence and sublimity of the prospect.

To the east, spread nearly all the rich vale of Eden, terminated by the Stainmore hills and other highlands of Yorkshire; to the northeast, the mountains of Cross-fell bounded the long landscape. The nearer grounds were Whinfield-park, broken, towards the Emont, into shrubby steeps, where the deep red of the soil mingled with the verdure of foliage; part of Sir Michael le Fleming's woods rounding a hill on the opposite bank, and, beyond, a wide extent of low land.[39] To the south, swelled the upland boundaries of Bamptonvale, with Lowther-woods, shading the pastures and distantly crowned by the fells of Haweswater; more to the west, Bird's Nest, 'bosomed high in tufted trees;'[40] at its foot, Lowther-bridge, and, a little further, the neat hamlet and bridge of Emont. In the low lands, still nearer, the Lowther and Emont united, the latter flowing in shining circles among the woods and deep-green meadows of Carleton-park. Beyond, at a vast distance to the west and north, rose all the alps of all the lakes! an horizon scarcely to be equalled in England. Among these broken mountains, the shaggy ridge of Saddleback was proudly pre-eminent; but one forked top of its rival Skiddaw peeped over its declining side. Helvellyn, huge and mis-shapen, towered above the fells of Ullswater. The sun's rays, streaming from beneath a line of dark clouds, that overhung the west, gave a tint of silvery light to all these alps, and reminded us of the first exquisite appearance of the mountains, at Goodesberg, which, however, in grandeur and elegance of outline, united with picturesque richness, we have never seen equalled.

Of the walls around us every ledge, marking their many stories, was embossed with luxuriant vegetation. Tufts of the hawthorn seemed to grow from the solid stone, and slender saplings of ash waved over the deserted door-cases, where, at the transforming hour of twilight, the superstitious eye might mistake them for spectres of some early possessor of the castle, restless from guilt, or of some sufferer persevering from vengeance.

THE TOWN AND BEACON OF PENRITH

HAVING PURSUED the road one mile further, for the purpose of visiting the tender memorial of pious affection, so often described under the name of Countess' Pillar, we returned to Emont-bridge, and from thence reached Penrith, pronounced Peyrith, the most southern town of Cumberland.[41] So far off as the head of Ullswater, fourteen miles, this is talked of as an important place, and looked to as the storehouse of whatever is wanted more than the fields and lakes supply. Those, who have lived chiefly in large towns, have to learn from the wants and dependencies of a people thinly scattered, like the inhabitants of all mountainous regions, the great value of any places of mutual resort, however little distinguished in the general view of a country. Penrith is so often mentioned in the neighbourhood, that the first appearance of it somewhat disappointed us, because we had not considered how many serious reasons those, who talked of it, might have for their estimation, which should yet not at all relate to the qualities, that render places interesting to a traveller.

The town, consisting chiefly of old houses, straggles along two sides of the high north road, and is built upon the side of a mountain, that towers to great height above it, in steep and heathy knolls, unshaded by a single tree. Eminent, on the summit of this mountain, stands the old, solitary beacon, visible from almost every part of Penrith, which, notwithstanding its many symptoms of antiquity, is not deficient of neatness. The houses are chiefly white, with door and window cases of the red stone found in the neighbourhood. Some of the smaller have over their doors dates of the latter end of the sixteenth century. There are several inns, of which that called Old Buchanan's was recommended to us, first, by the recollection, that Mr. Gray had mentioned it, and afterwards by the comfort and civility we found there.[42]

Some traces of the Scottish dialect and pronunciation appear as far south as Lancashire; in Westmoreland, they become stronger; and, at Penrith, are extremely distinct and general, serving for one among many peaceful indications of an approach, once notified chiefly by preparations for hostility, or defence. Penrith is the most southern town in England at which the guinea notes of the Scotch bank are in circulation. The beacon, a sort of square tower, with a peaked roof and openings at the sides, is a more perfect instance of the direful necessities of past ages, than would be expected to remain in this. The circumstances are well known, which made such watchfulness especially proper, at Penrith; and the other traces of warlike habits and precautions, whether appearing in records, or buildings, are too numerous to be noticed in a sketch, which rather pretends to describe what the author has seen, than to enumerate what has been discovered by the researches of others. Dr. Burn's History contains many curious particulars;[43] and there are otherwise abundant and satisfactory memorials, as to the state of the debateable ground, the regulations for securing passes or fords, and even to the public maintenance of slough dogs, which were to pursue aggressors with hot trod, as the inhabitants were to follow them by horn and voice.[44] These are all testimonies, that among the many evils, inflicted upon countries by war, that, which is not commonly thought of, is not the least; the public encouragement of a disposition to violence, under the names of gallantry, or valour, which will not cease exactly when it is publicly prohibited; and the education of numerous bodies to habits of supplying their wants, not by constant and useful labour, but by sudden and destructive exertions of force. The mistake, by which courage is released from all moral estimation of the purposes, for which it is exerted, and is considered to be necessarily and universally a good in itself, rather than a means of good, or of evil, according to its application, is among the severest misfortunes of mankind. Tacitus has an admirable reproof of it—

'Ubi manu agitur, modestia et probitas nomina superioris sunt.[45]

Though the situation of Penrith, looking up the vales of Eden and Emont, is remarkably pleasant, that of the beacon above is infinitely finer, commanding an horizon of at least an hundred miles diameter, filled with an endless variety of beauty, greatness and sublimity. The view extends over Cumberland, parts of Westmoreland, Lancashire, Yorkshire, and a corner of Northumberland and Durham. On a clear day, the Scottish high lands, beyond Solway Firth, may be distinguished, like faint clouds, on the horizon, and the steeples of Carlisle are plainly visible. All the intervening country, speckled with towns and villages, is spread beneath the eye, and, nearly eighty miles to the eastward, part of the Cheviot-hills are traced, a dark line, binding the distance and marking the separation between earth and sky. On the plains towards Carlisle, the nearer ridges of Cross-fell are seen to commence, and thence stretch their barren steeps thirty miles towards the east, where they disappear among the Stainmore hills and the huge moorlands of Yorkshire, that close up the long landscape of the vale of Eden. Among these, the broken lines of Ingleborough start above all the broader ones of the moors, and that mountain still proclaims itself sovereign of the Yorkshire heights.

Southward, rise the wonders of Westmoreland, Shapfells, ridge over ridge, the nearer pikes of Haweswater, and then the mountains of Ullswater, Helvellyn pre-eminent amongst them, distinguished by the grandeur and boldness of their outline, as well as the variety of their shapes; some hugely swelling, some aspiring in clusters of alpine points, and some broken into shaggy ridges. The sky, westward from hence and far to the north, displays a vision of Alps, Saddleback spreading towards Keswick its long shattered ridge, and one top of Skiddaw peering beyond it; but the others of this district are inferior in grandeur to the fells of Ullswater, more broken into points, and with less of contrast in their forms. Behind Saddleback, the skirts of Skiddaw spread themselves, and thence low hills shelve into the plains of Cumberland, that extend to Whitehaven; the only level line in the scope of this vast horizon. The scenery nearer to the eye exhibited cultivation in its richest state, varied with pastoral and sylvan beauty; landscapes embellished by the elegancies of art, and rendered venerable by the ruins of time. In the vale of Eden, Carleton-hall, flourishing under the hand of careful attention, and Bird's Nest, luxuriant in its spiry woods, opposed their cheerful beauties to the neglected walls of Brougham Castle, once the terror, and, even in ruins, the pride of the scene, now half-shrouded in its melancholy grove. These objects were lighted up by partial gleams of sunshine, which, as they fled along the valley, gave magical effect to all they touched.

The other vales in the home prospect were those of Bampton and Emont; the first open and gentle, shaded by the gradual woods of Lowther-park; the last closer and more romantic, withdrawing in many a lingering bend towards

Ullswater, where it is closed by the pyramidal Dunmallard, but not before a gleam of the lake is suffered to appear beyond the dark base of the hill. At the nearer end of the vale, and immediately under the eye, the venerable ruins of Penrith Castle crest a round green hill. These are of pale-red stone, and stand in detached masses; but have little that is picturesque in their appearance, time having spared neither tower, or gateway, and not a single tree giving shade, or force, to the shattered walls. The ground about the castle is broken into grassy knolls, and only cattle wander over the desolated tract. Time has also obscured the name of the founder; but it is known, that the main building was repaired, and some addition made to it by Richard the Third, when Duke of Gloucester, who lived here, for five years, in his office of sheriff of Cumberland, promoting the York interest by artful hospitalities, and endeavouring to strike terror into the Lancastrians. Among the ruins is a subterraneous passage, leading to a house in Penrith, above three hundred yards distant, called Dockwray Castle. The town lies between the fortress and the Beacon-hill, spreading prettily along the skirts of the mountain, with its many roofs of blue slate, among which the church rises near a dark grove.

Penrith, from the latter end of the last century, till lately, when it was purchased by the Duke of Devonshire, belonged to the family of Portland, to whom it was given by William the Third; probably instead of the manors in Wales, which it was one of William's few faulty designs to have given to his favourite companion, had not Parliament remonstrated, and informed him, that the Crown could not alienate the territories of the Principality. The church, a building of red stone, unusually well disposed in the interior, is a vicarage of small endowment; but the value of money in this part of the kingdom is so high, that the merit of independence, a merit and a happiness which should always belong to clergymen, is attainable by the possessors of very moderate incomes. What is called the Giant's Grave in the church yard is a narrow spot, inclosed, to the length of fourteen or fifteen feet, by rows of low stones, at the sides, and, at the ends, by two pillars, now slender, but apparently worn by the weather from a greater thickness. The height of these is eleven or twelve feet; and all the stones, whether in the borders, at the sides, or in these pillars, bear traces of rude carving, which shew, at least, that the monument must have been thought very important by those that raised it, since the singularity of its size was not held a sufficient distinction. We pored intently over these traces, though certainly without the hope of discovering any thing not known to the eminent antiquarians, who have confessed their ignorance concerning the origin of them.

FROM PENRITH TO KESWICK

THE GRAYSTOCK ROAD, which we took for the first five or six miles, is uninteresting, and offers nothing worthy of attention, before the approach to the castle, the seat of the Duke of Norfolk. The appearance of this from the road is good; a gray building, with gothic towers, seated in a valley among lawns and woods, that stretch, with great pomp of shade, to gently-rising hills. Behind these, Saddleback, huge, gray and barren, rises with all its ridgy lines; a grand and simple back-ground, giving exquisite effect to the dark woods below. Such is the height of the mountain, that, though eight or ten miles off, it appeared, as we approached the castle, almost to impend over it. Southward from Saddleback, a multitude of pointed summits crowd the horizon; and it is most interesting, after leaving Graystock, to observe their changing attitudes, as you advance, and the gradual disclosure of their larger features. Perhaps, a sudden display of the sublimest scenery, however full, imparts less emotion, than a gradually increasing view of it; when expectation takes the highest tone, and imagination finishes the sketch.

About two miles beyond Graystock, the moorlands commence, and, as far as simple greatness constitutes sublimity, this was, indeed, a sublime prospect; less so only than that from Shapfell itself, where the mountains are not so varied in their forms and are plainer in their grandeur. We were on a vast plain, if plain that may be called, which swells into long undulations, surrounded by an amphitheatre of heathy mountains, that seem to have been shook by some grand convulsion of the earth, and tumbled around in all shapes. Not a tree, a hedge, and seldom even a stone wall, broke the grandeur of their lines; what was not heath was only rock and gray crags; and a shepherd's hut, or his flocks, browsing on the steep sides of the fells, or in the narrow vallies, that opened distantly, was all that diversified the vast scene. Saddleback spread his skirts westward along the plain, and then reared himself in terrible and lonely majesty. In the long perspective beyond, were the crowding points of the fells round Keswick, Borrowdale, and the vales of St. John and Legberthwaite, stretching away to those near Grasmere. The weather was in solemn harmony with the scenery; long shadows swept over the hills, followed by gleaming lights. Tempestuous gusts alone broke the silence. Now and then, the sun's rays had a singular appearance; pouring, from under clouds, between the tops of fells into some deep vale, at a distance, as into a focus.

This is the very region, which the wild fancy of a poet, like Shakespeare, would people with witches, and shew them at their incantations, calling spirits from the clouds and spectres from the earth.

On the now lonely plains of this vast amphitheatre, the Romans had two camps, and their Eagle spread its wings over a scene worthy of its own soarings. The lines of these encampments may still be traced on that part of the plain, called Hutton Moor, to the north of the high road; and over its whole extent towards Keswick a Roman way has been discovered. Funereal urns have also been dug up here, and an altar of Roman form, but with the inscription obliterated.

Nearer Saddleback, we perceived crags and heath mingling on its precipices, and its base broken into a little world of mountains, green with cultivation. White farms, each with its grove to shelter it from the descending gusts, corn and pastures of the brightest verdure enlivened the skirts of the mountain all round, climbing towards the dark heath and crags, or spreading downwards into the vale of Threlkeld, where the slender Lowther shews his shining stream.

Leaving Hutton Moor, the road soon began to ascend the skirts of Saddleback, and passed between green hillocks, where cattle appeared most elegantly in the mountain scene, under the crags, or sipping at the clear stream, that gushed from the rocks, and wound to the vale below. Such crystal rivulets crossed our way continually, as we rose upon the side of Saddleback, which towers abruptly on the right, and, on the left, sinks as suddenly into the vale of Threlkeld, with precipices sometimes little less than tremendous. This mountain is the northern boundary of the vale in its whole length to Keswick, the points of whose fells close the perspective. Rocky heights guard it to the south. The valley between is green, without wood, and, with much that is grand, has little beautiful, till near its conclusion; where, more fertile and still more wild, it divides into three narrower vallies, two of which disclose scenes of such sublime severity as even our long view of Saddleback had not prepared us to expect.

The first of these is the vale of St. John, a narrow, cultivated spot, lying in the bosom of tremendous rocks, that impend over it in masses of gray crag, and often resemble the ruins of castles. These rocks are overlooked by still more awful mountains, that fall in abrupt lines, and close up the vista, except where they also are commanded by the vast top of Helvellyn. On every side, are images of desolation and stupendous greatness, closing upon a narrow line of pastoral richness; a picture of verdant beauty, seen through a frame of rock work. It is between the cliffs of Threlkeld-fell and the purple ridge of Nadale-fell, that this vale seems to repose in its most silent and perfect peace. No village and scarcely a cottage disturbs its retirement. The flocks, that feed at the feet of the cliffs, and the steps of a shepherd, 'in this office of his mountain watch,' are all, that haunt the 'dark sequestered nook.'[46]

The vale of Nadale runs parallel with that of St. John, from which it is separated by the ridge of Nadale-fell, and has the same style of character, except that it is terminated by a well wooded mountain. Beyond this, the perspective is overlooked by the fells, that terminate the vale of St. John.

The third valley, opening from the head of Threlkeld, winds along the feet of Saddleback and Skiddaw to Keswick, the approach to which, with all its world of rocky summits, the lake being still sunk below the sight, is sublime beyond the power of description. Within three miles of Keswick, Skiddaw unfolds itself, close behind Saddleback; their skirts unite, but the former is less huge and of very different form from the last; being more pointed and seldomer broken into precipices, it darts upward with a vast sweep into three spiry summits, two of which only are seen from this road, and shews sides dark with heath and little varied with rock. Such is its aspect from the Penrith road; from other stations its attitude, shape and colouring are very different, though its alpine terminations are always visible.

Threlkeld itself is a small village, about thirteen miles from Penrith, with a very humble inn, at which those, who have passed the bleak sides of Saddleback, and those, who are entering upon them, may rejoice to rest. We had been blown about, for some hours, in an open chaise, and hoped for more refreshment than could be obtained; but had the satisfaction, which was, indeed, general in these regions, of observing the good intentions, amounting almost to kindness, of the cottagers towards their guests. They have nearly always some fare, which less civility than theirs might render acceptable; and the hearth blazes in their clean sanded parlours, within two minutes after you enter them. Some sort of preserved fruit is constantly served after the repast, with cream, an innocent luxury, for which no animal has died.

It is not only from those, who are to gain by strangers, but from almost every person, accidentally accosted by a question, that this favourable opinion will be formed, as to the kind and frank manners of the people. We were continually remarking, between Lancaster and Keswick, that severe as the winter might be in these districts, from the early symptoms of it then apparent, the conduct of the people would render it scarcely unpleasant to take the same journey in the depths of December.

In these countries, the farms are, for the most part, small, and the farmers and their children work in the same fields with their servants. Their families have thus no opportunities of temporary insight into the society, and luxuries of the great, and have none of those miseries, which dejected vanity and multiplied wishes inflict upon the pursuers of the higher ranks. They are also without the baseness, which such pursuers usually have, of becoming abject before persons of one class, that by the authority of an apparent connection with them, they may be insolent to those of another; and are free from the essential humiliation of shewing, by a general and undistinguishing admiration of all persons richer than themselves, that the original distinctions between virtue and vice have been erased from their minds by the habit of comparing the high and the low.

The true consciousness of independence, which labour and an ignorance of the vain appendages, falsely called luxuries, give to the inhabitants of these districts, is probably the cause of the superiority, perceived by strangers in their tempers and manners, over those of persons, apparently better circumstanced. They have no remembrance of slights, to be revenged by insults; no hopes from servility, nor irritation from the desire of unattainable distinctions. Where, on the contrary, the encouragement of artificial wants has produced dependence, and mingled with the fictitious appearance of wealth many of the most real evils of poverty, the benevolence of the temper flies with the simplicity of the mind. There is, perhaps, not a more odious prospect of human society, than where an ostentatious, manoeuvring and corrupted peasantry, taking those, who induce them to crimes, for the models of their morality, mimic the vices, to which they were not born, and attempt the coarse covering of cunning and insolence for practices, which it is a science and frequently an object of education to conceal by flagitious elegancies.[47] Such persons form in the country a bad copy of the worst London society; the vices, without the intelligence, and without the assuaging virtues.

DRUIDICAL MONUMENT

AFTER PASSING the very small, but neatly furnished church of Threlkeld, the condition of which may be one testimony to the worthiness of the neighbourhood, and rising beyond the vales before described, we came to the brow of a hill, called Castle Rigg, on which, to the left of the road, are the remains of one of those circular monuments, which, by general consent, are called Druids' Temples. This is formed of thirty-seven stones, placed in a circle of about twenty-eight yards diameter, the largest being not less than seven feet and a half high, which is double the height of the others. At the eastern part of this circle, and within it, smaller stones are arranged in an oblong of about seven yards long, and, at the greatest breadth, four yards wide. Many of those round the circle appear to have fallen and now remain at unequal distances, of which the greatest is towards the north.

Engraving of Druids' Stones near Keswick by Thomas Allom,
pub. Fisher, Son and Co, c. 1832

Whether our judgment was influenced by the authority of a Druid's choice, or that the place itself commanded the opinion, we thought this situation the most severely grand of any hitherto passed. There is, perhaps, not a single object in the scene, that interrupts the solemn tone of feeling, impressed by its general characters of profound solitude, greatness and awful wildness. Castle Rigg is the central point of three vallies, that dart immediately under it from the eye, and whose mountains form part of an amphitheatre, which is completed by those of Derwentwater, in the west, and by the precipices of Skiddaw and Saddleback, close on the north. The hue, which pervades all these mountains, is that of dark heath, or rock; they are thrown into every form and direction, that Fancy would suggest, and are at that distance, which allows all their grandeur to prevail; nearer than the high lands, that surround Hutton Moor, and further removed than the fells in the scenery of Ullswater.

To the south open the rocks, that disclose the vale of St. John, whose verdant beauty bears no proportion to its sublimity; to the west, are piled the shattered and fantastic points of Derwentwater; to the north, Skiddaw, with its double top, resembling a volcano, the cloudy vapours ascending from its highest point, like smoke, and sometimes rolling in wreaths down its sides; and to the east, the vale of Threlkeld, spreading green round the base of Saddleback, its vast side-skreen, opened to the moorlands, beyond which the ridge of Cross-fell appeared; its dignity now diminished by distance. This point then is surrounded by the three grand rivals of Cumberland; huge Helvellyn, spreading Saddleback and spiry Skiddaw.

Such seclusion and sublimity were, indeed, well suited to the deep and wild mysteries of the Druids. Here, at moon-light, every Druid, summoned by that terrible horn, never awakened but upon high occasions, and descending from his mountain, or secret cave, might assemble without intrusion from one sacrilegious footstep, and celebrate a midnight festival by a savage sacrifice—

—'rites of such strange potency
As, done in open day, would dim the sun,
Tho' thron'd in noontide brightness.'
Caractacus.

Here, too, the Bards,

'Rob'd in their flowing vests of innocent white,
Descend, with harps, that glitter to the moon,
Hymning immortal strains. The spirits of air,
Of earth, of water, nay of heav'n itself,
Do listen to their lay; and oft, 'tis said,
In visible shapes, dance they a magic round
To the high minstrelsy.' [48]

As we descended the steep mountain to Keswick, the romantic fells round the lake opened finely, but the lake itself was concealed, deep in its rocky cauldron. We saw them under the last glow of sun-set, the upward rays producing a misty purple glory between the dark tops of Cawsey-pikes and the bending peaks of Thornthwaite fells. Soon after, the sun having set to the vale of Keswick, there appeared, beyond breaks in its western mountains, the rocks of other vallies, still lighted up by a purple gleam, and receiving strong rays on shaggy points, to which their recesses gave soft and shadowy contrast. But the magical effect of these sunshine rocks, opposed to the darkness of the nearer valley, can scarcely be imagined.

Still as we descended, the lake of Derwentwater was screened from our view; but the rich level of three miles wide, that spreads between it and Bassenthwaite-water in the same vale, lay, like a map, beneath us, chequered with groves and cottages, with enclosures of corn and meadows, and adorned by the pretty village of Crossthwaite, its neat white church conspicuous among trees. The fantastic fells of Derwentwater bordered this reposing landscape, on the west, and the mighty Skiddaw rose over it, on the east, concealing the lake of Bassenthwaite.

The hollow dashings of the Greta, in its rocky channel, at the foot of Skiddaw, and in one of the most wizard little glens that nature ever fancied, were heard long before we looked down its steep woody bank, and saw it winding away, from close inaccessible chasms, to the vale of Keswick, corn and meadows spread at the top of the left bank, and the crags of Skiddaw scowling over it, on the right.

At length, we had a glimpse of the north end of Derwentwater, and soon after entered Keswick, a small place of stone houses, lying at the foot of Castle Rigg, near Skiddaw, and about a quarter of a mile from the lake, which, however, is not seen from the town.

Engraving of Derwentwater, pub. John Garnett, c. 1850

We were impatient to view this celebrated lake, and immediately walked down to Crow-park, a green eminence at its northern end, whence it is generally allowed to appear to great advantage. Expectation had been raised too high: Shall we own our disappointment? Prepared for something more than we had already seen, by what has been so eloquently said of it, by the view of its vast neighbourhood and the grandeur of its approach, the lake itself looked insignificant; and, however rude, or awful, its nearer rocks might have appeared, if seen unexpectedly, they were not in general so vast, or so boldly outlined, as to retain a character of sublimity from comparison. Opposed to the simple majesty of Ullswater, the lake of Derwent was scarcely interesting. Something must, indeed, be attributed to the force of first impressions; but, with all allowance for this, Ullswater must still retain an high pre-eminence for grandeur and sublimity.

Derwentwater, however, when more minutely viewed, has peculiar charms both from beauty and wildness, and as the emotions, excited by disappointed expectation, began to subside, we became sensible of them. It seems to be nearly of a round form, and the whole is seen at one glance, expanding within an amphitheatre of mountains, rocky, but not vast, broken into many fantastic shapes, peaked, splintered, impending, sometimes pyramidal, opening by narrow vallies to the view of rocks, that rise immediately beyond and are again overlooked by others. The precipices seldom overshoot the water, but are arranged at some distance, and the shores swell with woody eminences, or sink into green, pastoral margins. Masses of wood also frequently appear among the cliffs, feathering them to their summits, and a white cottage sometimes peeps from out their skirts, seated on the smooth knoll of a pasture, projecting to the lake, and looks so exquisitely picturesque, as to seem placed there purposely to adorn it. The lake in return faithfully reflects the whole picture, and so even and brilliantly translucent is its surface, that it rather heightens, than obscures the colouring. Its mild bosom is spotted by four small islands, of which those called Lords' and St. Herbert's are well wooded, and adorn the scene, but another is deformed by buildings, stuck over it, like figures upon a twelfthcake.[49]

Beyond the head of the lake, and at a direct distance of three or four miles from Crow-park, the pass of Borrowdale opens, guarded by two piles of rock, the boldest in the scene, overlooked by many rocky points, and, beyond all, by rude mountain tops which come partially and in glimpses to the view. Among the most striking features of the eastern shore are the woody cliffs of Lowdore; then, nearer to the eye, Wallow-crags, a title used here as well as at Haweswater, of dark brown rock, loosely impending; nearer still, Castle-hill, pyramidal and richly wooded to its point, the most luxuriant feature of the landscape. Cawsey-pike, one of the most remarkable rocks of the western shore, has its ridge scolloped into points as if with a row of corbels.

The cultivated vale of Newland slopes upward from the lake between these and Thornthwaite fells. Northward, beyond Crow-park, rises Skiddaw; at its base commences the beautiful level, that spreads to Bassenthwaite-water, where the rocks in the west side of the perspective soon begin to soften, and the vale becomes open and cheerful.

Such is the outline of Derwentwater, which has a much greater proportion of beauty, than Ullswater, but neither its dignity, nor grandeur. Its fells, broken into smaller masses, do not swell, or start, into such bold lines as those of Ullswater; nor does the size of the lake accord with the general importance of the rocky vale, in which it lies. The water is too small for its accompaniments; and its form, being round and seen entirely at once, leaves nothing for expectation to pursue, beyond the stretching promontory, or fancy to transform within the gloom and obscurity of the receding fell; and thus it loses an ample source of the sublime. The greatest breadth from east to west is not more than three miles. It is not large enough to occupy the eye, and it is not so hidden as to have the assistance of the imagination in making it appear large. The beauty of its banks also, contending with the wildness of its rocks, gives opposite impressions to the mind, and the force of each is, perhaps, destroyed by the admission of the other. Sublimity can scarcely exist, without simplicity; and even grandeur loses much of its elevating effect, when united with a considerable portion of beauty; then descending to become magnificence. The effect of simplicity in assisting that high tone of mind, produced by the sublime, is demonstrated by the scenery of Ullswater, where very seldom a discordant object obtrudes over the course of thought, and jars upon the feelings.

But it is much pleasanter to admire than to examine, and in Derwentwater is abundant subject for admiration, though not of so high a character as that, which attends Ullswater. The soft undulations of its shores, the mingled wood and pasture, that paint them, the brilliant purity of the water, that gives back every landscape on its bank, and frequently with heightened colouring, the fantastic wildness of the rocks and the magnificence of the amphitheatre they form; these are circumstances, the view of which excites emotions of sweet, though tranquil admiration, softening the mind to tenderness, rather than elevating it to sublimity. We first saw the whole beneath such sober hues as prevailed when

'the gray hooded Even,
Like a sad votarist, in Palmer's weed,
Rose from the hindmost wheels of Phoebus' wain.'

The wildness, seclusion, and magical beauty of this vale, seem, indeed, to render it the very abode for Milton's Comus, 'deep skilled in all his mother's witcheries;' and, while we survey its fantastic features, we are almost tempted to suppose, that he has hurled his

'dazzling spells into the air,
Of power to cheat the eye with blear illusion
And give it false presentments.'

Nay more, to believe

'All the sage poets, taught by th' heavenly muse
Storied of old, in high immortal verse,
Of dire chimaeras and enchanted isles;'

and to fancy we hear from among the woody cliffs, near the shore,

'the sound
Of riot and ill manag'd merriment,'

succeeded by such strains as oft

'in pleasing slumbers lull the sense,
And, in sweet madness, rob it of itself.'[50]

SKIDDAW

O N THE FOLLOWING MORNING, having engaged a guide, and with horses accustomed to the labour, we began to ascend this tremendous mountain by a way, which makes the summit five miles from Keswick.[51] Passing through bowery lanes, luxuriant with mountain ash, holly, and a variety of beautiful shrubs, to a broad, open common, a road led us to the foot of Latrigg, or, as it is called by the country people, Skiddaw's Cub, a large round hill, covered with heath, turf and browsing sheep. A narrow path now wound along steep green precipices, the beauty of which prevented what danger there was from being perceived. Derwentwater was concealed by others, that rose above them, but that part of the vale of Keswick, which separates the two lakes, and spreads a rich level of three miles, was immediately below; Crossthwaite-church, nearly in the centre, with the white vicarage, rising among trees. More under shelter of Skiddaw, where the vale spreads into a sweet retired nook, lay the house and grounds of Dr. Brownrigg.[52]

Beyond the level, opened a glimpse of Bassenthwaite-water; a lake, which may be called elegant, bounded, on one side, by well wooded rocks, and, on the other, by Skiddaw.

Soon after, we rose above the steeps, which had concealed Derwentwater, and it appeared, with all its enamelled banks, sunk deep amidst a chaos of mountains, and surrounded by ranges of fells, not visible from below. On the other hand, the more cheerful lake of Bassenthwaite expanded at its entire length. Having gazed a while on this magnificent scene, we pursued the path, and soon after reached the brink of a chasm, on the opposite side of which wound our future track; for the ascent is here in an acutely zig-zag direction. The horses carefully picked their steps along the narrow precipice, and turned the angle, that led them to the opposite side.

At length, as we ascended, Derwentwater dwindled on the eye to the smallness of a pond, while the grandeur of its amphitheatre was increased by new ranges of dark mountains, no longer individually great, but so from accumulation; a scenery to give ideas of the breaking up of a world. Other precipices soon hid it again, but Bassenthwaite continued to spread immediately below us, till we turned into the heart of Skiddaw, and were enclosed by its steeps. We had now lost all track even of the flocks, that were scattered over these tremendous wilds. The guide conducted us by many curvings among the heathy hills and hollows of the mountain; but the ascents were such, that the horses panted in the slowest walk, and it was necessary to let them rest every six or seven minutes. An opening to the south, at length, shewed the whole plan of the narrow vales of St. John and of Nadale, separated by the dark ridge of rock, called St. John's-rigg, with each its small line of verdure at the bottom, and bounded by enormous gray fells, which we were, however, now high enough to overlook.

A white speck, on the top of St. John's rigg, was pointed out by the guide to be a chapel of ease to Keswick, which has no less than five such scattered among the fells. From this chapel, dedicated to St. John, the rock and the vale have received their name, and our guide told us, that Nadale was frequently known by the same title.

Leaving this view, the mountain soon again shut out all prospect, but of its own vallies and precipices, covered with various shades of turf and moss, and with heath, of which a dull purple was the prevailing hue. Not a tree, or bush appeared on Skiddaw, nor even a stone wall any where broke the simple greatness of its lines. Sometimes, we looked into tremendous chasms, where the torrent, heard roaring long before it was seen, had worked itself a deep channel, and fell from ledge to ledge, foaming and shining amidst the dark rock. These streams are sublime from the length and precipitancy of their course, which, hurrying the sight with them into the abyss, act, as it were, in sympathy upon the nerves, and, to save ourselves from following, we recoil from the view with involuntary horror. Of such, however, we saw only two, and those by some departure from the usual course up the mountain; but every where met gushing springs, till we were within two miles of the summit, when our guide added to the rum in his bottle what he said was the last water we should find in our ascent.

The air now became very thin, and the steeps still more difficult of ascent; but it was often delightful to look down into the green hollows of the mountain, among pastoral scenes, that wanted only some mixture of wood to render them enchanting.

About a mile from the summit, the way was, indeed, dreadfully sublime, laying, for nearly half a mile, along the ledge of a precipice, that passed, with a swift descent, for probably near a mile, into a glen within the heart of Skiddaw; and not a bush, or a hillock interrupted its vast length, or, by offering a midway check in the descent, diminished the fear it inspired. The ridgy steeps of Saddleback formed the opposite boundary of the glen, and, though really at a considerable distance, had, from the height of the two mountains, such an appearance of nearness, that it almost seemed as if we could spring to its side. How much too did simplicity increase the sublime of this scenery, in which nothing but mountain, heath and sky appeared.

But our situation was too critical, or too unusual, to permit the just impressions of such sublimity. The hill rose so closely above the precipice as scarcely to allow a ledge wide enough for a single horse. We followed the guide in silence, and, till we regained the more open wild, had no leisure for exclamation. After this, the ascent appeared easy and secure, and we were bold enough to wonder, that the steeps near the beginning of the mountain had excited any anxiety.

At length, passing the skirts of the two points of Skiddaw, which are nearest to Derwentwater, we approached the third and loftiest, and then perceived, that their steep sides, together with the ridges, which connect them, were entirely covered near the summits with a whitish shivered slate, which threatens to slide down them with every gust of wind. The broken state of this slate makes the present summits seem like the ruins of others; a circumstance as extraordinary in appearance as difficult to be accounted for.

The ridge, on which we passed from the neighbourhood of the second summit to the third, was narrow, and the eye reached, on each side, down the whole extent of the mountain, following, on the left, the rocky precipices, that impend over the lake of Bassenthwaite, and looking, on the right, into the glens of Saddleback, far, far below. But the prospects, that burst upon us from every part of the vast horizon, when we had gained the summit, were such as we had scarcely dared to hope for, and must now rather venture to enumerate, than to describe.

We stood on a pinnacle, commanding the whole dome of the sky. The prospects below, each of which had been before considered separately as a great scene, were now miniature parts of the immense landscape. To the north, lay, like a map, the vast tract of low country, which extends between Bassenthwaite and the Irish Channel, marked with the silver circles of the river Derwent, in its progress from the lake. Whitehaven and its white coast were distinctly seen, and Cockermouth seemed almost under the eye. A long blackish line, more to the west, resembling a faintly formed cloud, was said by the guide to be the Isle of Man, who, however, had the honesty to confess, that the mountains of Down in Ireland, which have been sometimes thought visible, had never been seen by him in the clearest weather.

Bounding the low country to the north, the wide Solway Firth, with its indented shores, looked like a gray horizon, and the double range of Scottish mountains, seen dimly through mist beyond, like lines of dark clouds above it. The Solway appeared surprisingly near us, though at fifty miles distance, and the guide said, that, on a bright day, its shipping could plainly be discerned. Nearly in the north, the heights seemed to soften into plains, for no object was there visible through the obscurity, that had begun to draw over the furthest distance; but, towards the east, they appeared to swell again, and what we were told were the Cheviot hills dawned feebly beyond Northumberland. We now spanned the narrowest part of England, looking from the Irish Channel, on one side, to the German Ocean, on the other, which latter was, however, so far off as to be discernible only like a mist.[53]

Nearer than the county of Durham, stretched the ridge of Crossfell, and an indistinct multitude of the Westmoreland and Yorkshire highlands, whose lines disappeared behind Saddleback, now evidently pre-eminent over Skiddaw, so much so as to exclude many a height beyond it. Passing this mountain in our course to the south, we saw, immediately below, the fells round Derwentwater, the lake itself remaining still concealed in their deep rocky bosom. Southward and westward, the whole prospect was a 'turbulent chaos of dark mountains.'[54] All individual dignity was now lost in the immensity of the whole, and every variety of character was overpowered by that of astonishing and gloomy grandeur.

Over the fells of Borrowdale, and far to the south, the northern end of Windermere appeared, like a wreath of gray smoke, that spreads along the mountain's side. More southward still, and beyond all the fells of the lakes, Lancaster sands extended to the faintly seen waters of the sea. Then to the west, Duddon sands gleamed in a long line among the fells of High Furness.

Immediately under the eye, lay Bassenthwaite, surrounded by many ranges of mountains, invisible from below. We overlooked all these dark mountains, and saw green cultivated vales over the tops of lofty rocks, and other mountains over these vales in many ridges, whilst innumerable narrow glens were traced in all their windings and seen uniting behind the hills with others, that also sloped upwards from the lake.

The air on this summit was boisterous, intensely cold and difficult to be inspired, though the day was below warm and serene. It was dreadful to look down from nearly the brink of the point, on which we stood, upon the lake of Bassenthwaite and over a sharp and separated ridge of rocks, that from below appeared of tremendous height, but now seemed not to reach half way up Skiddaw; it was almost as if

'the precipitation might down stretch
Below the beam of sight.'[55]

Under the lee of an heaped up pile of slates, formed by the customary contribution of one from every visitor, we found an old man sheltered, whom we took to be a shepherd, but afterwards learned was a farmer and, as the people in this neighbourhood say, a 'statesman;' that is, had land of his own. He was a native and still an inhabitant of an adjoining vale; but, so laborious is the enterprise reckoned, that, though he had passed his life within view of the mountain, this was his first ascent. He descended with us, for part of our way, and then wound off towards his own valley, stalking amidst the wild scenery, his large figure wrapt in a dark cloak and his steps occasionally assisted by a long iron pronged pike, with which he had pointed out distant objects.

In the descent, it was interesting to observe each mountain below gradually re-assuming its dignity, the two lakes expanding into spacious surfaces, the many little vallies, that sloped upwards from their margins, recovering their variegated tints of cultivation, the cattle again appearing in the meadows, and the woody promontories changing from smooth patches of shade into richly tufted summits. At about a mile from the top, a great difference was perceptible in the climate, which became comparatively warm, and the summer hum of bees was again heard among the purple heath.

We reached Keswick, about four o'clock, after five hours passed in this excursion, in which the care of our guide greatly lessened the notion of danger. Why should we think it trivial to attempt some service towards this poor man? We have reason to think, that whoever employs, at Keswick, a guide of the name of Doncaster, will assist him in supporting an aged parent.

BASSENTHWAITE WATER

IN A GRAY autumnal morning, we rode out along the western bank of Bassenthwaite to Ouse Bridge, under which the river Derwent, after passing through the lake, takes its course towards the Sea. The road on this side, being impassable by carriages, is seldom visited, but it is interesting for being opposed to Skiddaw, which rises in new attitudes over the opposite bank. Beyond the land, that separates the two lakes, the road runs high along the sides of hills and sometimes at the feet of tremendous fells, one of which rises almost spirally over it, shewing a surface of slates, shivered from top to bottom. Further on, the heights gradually soften from horror into mild and graceful beauty, opening distantly to the cheerful country, that spreads towards Whitehaven; but the road soon immerges among woods, which allow only partial views of the opposite shore, inimitably beautiful with copses, green lawns and pastures, with gently sweeping promontories and bays, that receive the lake to their full brims.

From the house at Ouse Bridge the prospect is exquisite up the lake, which now losing the air of a wide river, re-assumes its true character, and even appears to flow into the chasm of rocks, that really inclose Derwentwater. Skiddaw, with all the mountains round Borrowdale, form a magnificent amphitheatrical perspective for this noble sheet of water; the vallies of the two lakes extending to one view, which is, therefore, superior to any exhibited from Derwentwater alone. The prospect terminates in the dark fells of Borrowdale, which by their sublimity enhance the beauty and elegance, united to a surprising degree in the nearer landscape.

Beyond Ouse Bridge, but still at the bottom of the lake, the road passes before Armithwaite-house, whose copsy lawns slope to the margin of the water from a mansion more finely situated than any we had seen.[56] It then recedes somewhat from the bank, and ascends the skirt of Skiddaw, which it scarcely leaves on this side of Keswick. On the opposite shore, the most elegant features are the swelling hills, called Wythop-brows, flourishing with wood from the water's edge; and, below the meadows of the eastern bank, by which we were returning, two peninsulae, the one pastoral, yet well wooded and embellished by a white hamlet, the other narrow and bearing only a line of trees, issuing far into the lake. But the shores of Bassenthwaite, though elegant and often beautiful, are too little varied to be long dwelt upon; and attention is sometimes unpleasantly engaged by a precipice, from which the road is not sufficiently secured; so that the effect of the whole upon the imagination is much less than might be expected from its situation at the foot of Skiddaw, and its shape, which is more extended than that of Derwentwater.

BORROWDALE

A SERENE DAY, with gleams of sunshine, gave magical effect to the scenery of Derwentwater, as we wound along its eastern shore to Borrowdale, under cliffs, parts of which, already fallen near the road, increased the opinion of danger from the rest; sometimes near the edge of precipices, that bend over the water, and, at others, among pleasure-grounds and copses, which admit partial views over the lake. These, with every woody promontory and mountain, were perfectly reflected on its surface. Not a path-way, not a crag, or scar, that sculptured their bold fronts, but was copied and distinctly seen even from the opposite shore in the dark purple mirror below. Now and then, a pleasure-boat glided by, leaving long silver lines, drawn to a point on the smooth water, which, as it gave back the painted sides and gleaming sail, displayed a moving picture.

The colouring of the mountains was, this day, surprisingly various and changeful, surpassing every thing of the same nature, that we had seen. The effect of the atmosphere on mountainous regions is sometimes so sublime, at others so enchantingly beautiful, that the mention of it ought not to be considered as trivial, when their aspect is to be described. As the sun-beams fell on different kinds of rock, and distance coloured the air, some parts were touched with lilac, others with light blue, dark purple, or reddish brown, which were often seen, at the same moment, contrasting with the mellow green of the woods and the brightness of sunshine; then slowly and almost imperceptibly changing into other tints. Skiddaw itself exhibited much of this variety, during our ride. As we left Keswick, its points were overspread with pale azure; on our return, a tint of dark blue softened its features, which were, however, soon after involved in deepest purple.

Winding under the woods of Barrowside, we approached Lowdore, and heard the thunder of his cataract, joined by the sounds of others, descending within the gloom of the nearer rocks and thickets. The retrospective views over the lake from Barrowside are the finest in the ride; and, when the road emerges from the woods, a range of rocks rises over it, where many shrubs, and even oaks, ash, yew, grow in a surprising manner among the broken slates, that cover their sides. Beyond, at some distance from the shore, appear the awful rocks, that rise over the fall of Lowdore; that on the right shooting up, a vast pyramid of naked cliff, above finely wooded steeps; while, on the opposite side of the chasm, that receives the waters, impends Gowdar-crag, whose trees and shrubs give only shagginess to its terrible masses, with fragments of which the meadows below are strewn. There was now little water at Lowdore; but the breadth of its channel and the height of the perpendicular rock, from which it leaps, told how tremendous it could be; yet even then its sublimity is probably derived chiefly from the cliff and mountain, that tower closely over it.

Here Borrowdale begins, its rocks spreading in a vast sweep round the head of the lake, at the distance, perhaps, of half a mile from the shore, which bears meadow land to the water's brink. The aspect of these rocks, with the fragments, that have rolled from their summits, and lie on each side of the road, prepared us for the scene of tremendous ruin we were approaching in the gorge, or pass of Borrowdale, which opens from the centre of the amphitheatre, that binds the head of Derwentwater. Dark rocks yawn at its entrance, terrific as the wildness of a maniac; and disclose a narrow pass, running up between mountains of granite, that are shook into almost every possible form of horror. All above resembles the accumulations of an earthquake; splintered, shivered, piled, amassed. Huge cliffs have rolled down into the glen below, where, however, is still a miniature of the sweetest pastoral beauty, on the banks of the river Derwent; but description cannot paint either the wildness of the mountains, or the pastoral and sylvan peace and softness, that wind at their base.

Among the most striking of the fells are Glaramara, shewing rock on rock; and Eagle-crag, where, till lately, that bird built its nest; but the depredations, annually committed on its young, have driven it from the place.[57] Hence we pursued the pass for a mile, over a frightful road, that climbs among the crags of a precipice above the river, having frequently glimpses into glens and chasms, where all passage seemed to be obstructed by the fallen shivers of rock, and at length reached the gigantic stone of Bowther, that appears to have been pitched into the ground from the summit of a neighbouring fell, and is shaped, like the roof of a house reversed.

This is one of the spectacles of the country. Its size makes it impossible to have been ever moved by human means; and, if it fell from the nearest of the rocks, it must have rolled upon the ground much further than can be readily conceived of the motion of such a mass. The side towards the road projects about twelve feet over the base, and serves to shelter cattle in a penn, of which it is made to form one boundary. A small oak plant and a sloe have found soil enough to flourish in at the top; and the base is pitched on a cliff over the river, whence a long perspective of the gorge is seen, with a

Engraving of Bowder Stone by William Green, 1804

little level of bright verdure, spreading among more distant fells and winding away into trackless regions, where the mountains lift their ruffian heads in undisputed authority. Below, the shrunk Derwent serpentized along a wide bed of pebbles, that marked its wintry course, and left a wooded island, flourishing amidst the waste. The stillness around us was only feebly broken by the remote sounds of many unseen cataracts, and sometimes by the voices of mountaineer children, shouting afar off, and pleasing themselves with rousing the echoes of the rocks.

In returning, the view opened, with great magnificence, from the jaws of this pass over the lake to Skiddaw, then seen from its base, with the upper steeps of Saddleback obliquely beyond, and rearing itself far above all the heights of the eastern shore.[58] At the entrance of the gorge, the village or hamlet of Grange lies picturesquely on the bank of the Derwent among wood and meadows, and sheltered under the ruinous fell, called Castlecrag, that takes its name from the castle, or fortress, which from its crown once guarded this important pass.

Borrowdale abounds in valuable mines, among which some are known to supply the finest wadd, or black lead, to be found in England.[59] Iron, slate, and free stone of various kinds, are also the treasures of these mountains.

FROM KESWICK TO WINDERMERE

THE ROAD from Keswick to Ambleside commences by the ascent of Castle-rigg, the mountain, which the Penrith road descends, and which, on that side, is crowned by a Druid's temple. The rise is now very laborious, but the views it affords over the vale of Keswick are not dearly purchased by the fatigue. All Bassenthwaite, its mountains softening away in the perspective, and terminating, on the west, in the sister woods of Wythorp-brows, extends from the eye; and, immediately beneath, the northern end of Derwentwater, with Cawsey-pike, Thornthwaite-fell, the rich upland vale of Newland peeping from between their bases, and the spiry woods of Foepark jutting into the lake below. But the finest prospect is from a gate about halfway up the hill, whence you look down upon the head of Derwentwater, with all the alps of Borrowdale, opening darkly.

After descending Castle-rigg and crossing the top of St. John's vale, we seemed as if going into banishment from society, the road then leading over a plain, closely surrounded by mountains so wild, that neither a cottage, or a wood soften their rudeness, and so steep and barren, that not even sheep appear upon their sides. From this plain the road enters Legberthwaite, a narrow valley, running at the back of Borrowdale, green at the bottom, and varied with a few farms, but without wood, and with fells of gray precipices, rising to great height and nearly perpendicular on either hand, whose fronts are marked only by the torrents, that tumble from their utmost summits, and perpetually occur. We often stopped to listen to their hollow sounds amidst the solitary greatness of the scene, and to watch their headlong fall down the rocky chasms, their white foam and silver line contrasting with the dark hue of the clefts. In sublimity of descent these were frequently much superior to that of Lowdore, but as much inferior to it in mass of water and picturesque beauty.

As the road ascended towards Helvellyn, we looked back through this vast rocky vista to the sweet vale of St. John, lengthening the perspective, and saw, as through a telescope, the broad broken steeps of Saddleback and the points of Skiddaw, darkly blue, closing it to the north. The grand rivals of Cumberland were now seen together; and the road, soon winding high over the skirts of Helvellyn, brought us to Leathes-water, to which the mountain forms a vast side-skreen, during its whole length. This is a long, but narrow and unadorned lake, having little else than walls of rocky fells, starting from its margin. Continuing on the precipice, at some height from the shore, the road brought us, after three miles, to the poor village of Wythburn, and soon after to the foot of Dunmail Rays, which, though a considerable ascent, forms the dip of two lofty mountains, Steel-fell and Seat Sandle, that rise with finely-sweeping lines, on each side, and shut up the vale.

Beyond Dunmail Rays, one of the grand passes from Cumberland into Westmoreland, Helm-crag rears its crest, a strange fantastic summit, round, yet jagged and splintered, like the wheel of a water-mill, overlooking Grasmere, which, soon after, opened below. A green spreading circle of mountains embosoms this small lake, and, beyond, a wider range rises in amphitheatre, whose rocky tops are rounded and scolloped, yet are great, wild, irregular, and were then overspread with a tint of faint purple. The softest verdure margins the water, and mingles with corn enclosures and woods, that wave up the hills; but scarcely a cottage any where appears, except at the northern end of the lake, where the village of Grasmere and its very neat white church stand among trees, near the shore, with Helm-crag and a multitude of fells, rising over it and beyond each other in the perspective.

The lake was clear as glass, reflecting the headlong mountains, with every feature of every image on its tranquil banks; and one green island varies, but scarcely adorns its surface, bearing only a rude and now shadeless hut. At a considerable height above the water, the road undulates for a mile, till, near the southern end of Grasmere, it mounts the crags of a fell, and seemed carrying us again into such scenes of ruin and privation as we had quitted with Legberthwaite and Leathes-water. But, descending the other side of the mountain, we were soon cheered by the view of plantations, enriching the banks of Rydal-water, and by thick woods, mingling among cliffs above the narrow lake, which winds through a close valley, for about a mile. This lake is remarkable for the beauty of its small round islands, luxuriant with elegant trees and shrubs, and whose banks are green to the water's edge. Rydal-hall stands finely on an eminence, somewhat withdrawn from the east end, in a close romantic nook, among old woods, that feather the fells, which rise over their summits, and spread widely along the neighbouring eminences. This antient white mansion looks over a rough grassy descent, screened by groves of oak and majestic planes, towards the head of Windermere, about two miles distant, a small glimpse of which is caught beyond the wooded steeps of a narrow valley. In the woods and in the disposition of the ground round Rydal-hall there is a charming wildness, that suits the character of the general scene; and, wherever art appears, it is with graceful plainness and meek subjection to nature.

The taste, by which a cascade in the pleasure-grounds, pouring under the arch of a rude bridge, amidst the green tint of woods, is shewn through a darkened garden-house, and, therefore, with all the effect, which the opposition of light and shade can give, is even not too artificial; so admirably is the intent accomplished of making all the light, that is admitted, fall upon the objects, which are chiefly meant to be observed.

The road to Ambleside runs through the valley in front of Rydal-hall, and for some distance among the grounds that belong to it, where again the taste of the owner is conspicuous in the disposition of plantations among pastures of extraordinary richness, and where pure rivulets are suffered to wind without restraint over their dark rocky channels. Woods mantle up the cliffs on either side of this sweet valley, and, higher still, the craggy summits of the fells crowd over the scene. Two miles among its pleasant shades, near the banks of the murmuring Rotha, brought us to Ambleside, a black and very antient little town, hanging on the lower steeps of a mountain, where the vale opens to the head of

WINDERMERE

WHICH APPEARED at some distance below, in gentle yet stately beauty; but its boundaries shewed nothing of the sublimity and little of the romantic wildness, that charms, or elevates in the scenery of the other lakes. The shores, and the hills, which gradually ascend from them, are in general richly cultivated, or wooded, and correctly elegant; and when we descended upon the bank the road seemed leading through the artificial shades of pleasure-grounds. It undulates for two miles over low promontories and along spacious bays, full to their fringed margin with the abundance of this expansive lake; then, quitting the bank, it ascends gradual eminences, that look upon the vast plain of water, and rise amidst the richest landscapes of its shores. The manners of the people would have sufficiently informed us that Windermere is the lake most frequented; and with the great sublimity of the more sequestered scenes, we had to regret the interesting simplicity of their inhabitants, a simplicity which accorded so beautifully with the dignified character of the country. The next day, we visited several of the neighbouring heights, whence the lake is seen to great advantage; and, on the following, skirted the eastern shore for six miles to the Ferry.

Windermere, above twelve miles long and generally above a mile broad, but sometimes two, sweeps like a majestic river with an easy bend between low points of land and eminences that, shaded with wood and often embellished with villas, swell into hills cultivated to their summits; except that, for about six miles along the middle of the western shore, a range of rocky fells rise over the water. But these have nothing either picturesque or fantastic in their shape; they are heavy, not broken into parts, and their rudeness softens into insignificance, when they are seen over the wide channel of the lake; they are neither large enough to be grand, or wooded enough to be beautiful. To the north, or head of Windermere, however, the tameness of its general character disappears, and the scene soars into grandeur. Here, over a ridge of rough brown hills above a woody shore, rise, at the distance of a mile and half, or two miles, a multitude of finely alpine mountains, retiring obliquely in the perspective, among which Langdale-pikes, Hardknot and Wry-nose, bearing their bold, pointed promontories aloft, are pre-eminent. The colouring of these mountains, which are some of the grandest of Cumberland and Westmoreland, was this day remarkably fine. The weather was showery, with gleams of sunshine; sometimes their tops were entirely concealed in gray vapours, which, drawing upwards, would seem to ascend in volumes of smoke from their summits; at others, a few scattered clouds wandered along their sides, leaving their heads unveiled and effulgent with light. These clouds disappearing before the strength of the sun, a fine downy hue of light blue overspread the peeping points of the most distant fells, while the nearer ones were tinged with deep purple, which was opposed to the brown heath and crag of the lower hills, the olive green of two wooded slopes that, just tinted by autumn, seemed to descend to the margin, and the silver transparency of the expanding water at their feet. This view of Windermere appears with great majesty from a height above Culgarth, a seat of the Bishop of Landaff;[60] while, to the south, the lake after sweeping about four miles gradually narrows and disappears behind the great island, which stretches across the perspective.

At the distance of two or three miles beyond Culgarth, from a hill advancing towards the water, the whole of Windermere is seen; to the right, is the white mansion at Culgarth, among wood, on a gentle eminence of the shore, with the lake spreading wide beyond, crowned by the fells half obscured in clouds. To the south, the hills of the eastern shore, sloping gradually, run out in elegant and often well wooded points into the water, and are spotted with villas and varied above with enclosures. The opposite shore is for about a mile southward a continuation of the line of rock before noticed, from which Rawlinson's-nab pushes a bold headland over the lake; the perspective then sinks away in low hills, and is crossed by a remote ridge, that closes the scene.

The villages of Rayrig and Bowness, which are passed in the way to the Ferry, both stand delightfully; one on an eminence commanding the whole lake, and the other within a recess of the shore, nearly opposite the large island. The winding banks of Windermere continually open new landscapes as you move along them, and the mountains, which crown its head, are as frequently changing their attitudes; but Langdale-pikes, the boldest features in the scene, are soon lost to the eye behind the nearer fells of the western shore.

The ferry is considerably below Christian's island, and at the narrowest span of the lake, where two points of the shore extend to meet each other. This island, said to contain thirty acres, intermingled with wood, lawn and shrubberies, embellishes, without decreasing the dignity of the scene; it is surrounded by attendant islets, some rocky, but others, beautifully covered with wood, seem to coronet the flood.

In crossing the water the illusions of vision give force to the northern mountains, which viewed from hence appear to ascend from its margin and to spread round it in a magnificent amphitheatre. This was to us the most interesting view on Windermere.

On our approaching the western shore, the range of rocks that form it, discovered their cliffs, and gradually assumed a consequence, which the breadth of the channel had denied them; and their darkness was well opposed by the bright verdure and variegated autumnal tints of the isles at their base. On the bank, under shelter of these rocks, a white house was seen beyond the tall boles of a most luxuriant grove of plane-trees, which threw their shadows over it, and on the margin of the silver lake spreading in front. From hence the road ascends the steep and craggy side of Furness-fell, on the brow of which we had a last view of Windermere, in its whole course; to the south, its tame but elegant landscapes gliding away into low and long perspective, and the lake gradually narrowing; to the north, its more impressive scenery; but the finest features of it were now concealed by a continuation of the rocks we were upon.

Windermere is distinguished from all the other lakes of this country by its superior length and breath, by the gentle hills, cultivated and enclosed nearly to their summits, that generally bind its shores, by the gradual distance and fine disposition of the northern mountains, by the bold sweeps of its numerous bays, by the villas that speckle and rich plantations that wind them, and by one large island, surrounded by many islets, which adds dignity to its bosom. On the other lakes the islands are prettinesses, that do not accord with the character of the scene; they break also the surface of the water where vast continuity is required; and the mind cannot endure to descend suddenly from the gigantic sublimity of nature to her fairy sports. Yet, on the whole, Windermere was to us the least impressive of all the lakes. Except to the north, where the retiring mountains are disposed with uncommon grandeur of outline and magnificence of colouring, its scenery is tame, having little of the wild and nothing of the astonishing energy that appears on the features of the more sequestered districts. The characters of the three great lakes may, perhaps, be thus distinguished:

Windermere: Diffusiveness, stately beauty, and, at the upper end, magnificence.

Ullswater: Severe grandeur and sublimity; all that may give ideas of vast power and astonishing majesty. The effect of Ullswater is, that, awful as its scenery appears, it awakens the mind to expectation still more awful, and, touching all the powers of imagination, inspires that 'fine phrensy' descriptive of the poet's eye, which not only bodies forth unreal forms, but imparts to substantial objects a character higher than their own.[61]

Derwentwater: Fantastic wildness and romantic beauty, but inferior to Ullswater in greatness, both of water and rocks; for, though it charms and elevates, it does not display such features and circumstances of the sublime, or call up such expectation of unimaged and uncertain wonder. A principal defect, if we may venture to call it so, of Derwentwater is, that the water is too small in proportion for the amphitheatre of the valley in which it lies, and therefore loses much of the dignity, that in other circumstances it would exhibit. The fault of Windermere is, perhaps, exactly the reverse; where the shores, not generally grand, are rendered tamer by the ample expanse of the lake. The proportions of Ullswater are more just, and, though its winding form gives it in some parts the air of a river, the abrupt and tremendous height of its rocks, the dark and crowding summits of the fells above, the manner in which they enclose it, together with the dignity of its breadth, empower it constantly to affect the mind with emotions of astonishment and lofty expectation.

FROM WINDERMERE TO HAWKSHEAD, THURSTON-LAKE AND ULVERSTON[62]

AFTER ASCENDING the laborious crags and precipices of Furness-fell, enlivened, however, by frequent views of the southern end of Windermere, the road immediately descends the opposite side of the mountain, which shuts out the beautiful scenery of the lake; but the prospect soon after opens to other mountains of Furness, in the distance, which revive the expectation of such sublimity as we had lately regretted, and to Esthwait-water in the valley below. This is a narrow, pleasant lake, about half a mile broad and two miles long, with gradual hills, green to their tops, rising round the margin; with plantations and pastures alternately spreading along the easy shores and white farms scattered sparingly upon the slopes above. The water seems to glide through the quiet privacy of pleasure-grounds; so fine is the turf on its banks, so elegant its copses, and such an air of peace and retirement prevails over it. A neat white village lies at the feet of the hills near the head of the lake; beyond it is the gray town of Hawkshead, with its church and parsonage on an eminence commanding the whole valley. Steep hills rise over them, and, more distant, the tall heads of the Coniston-fells, dark and awful, with a confusion of other mountains.

Hawkshead, thus delightfully placed, is an antient, but small town, with a few good houses, and a neat town-house, lately built by subscriptions, of which the chief part was gratefully supplied by London merchants, who had been educated at the free school here; and this school itself is a memorial of gratitude, having been founded by Archbishop Sandys for the advantage of the town, which gave him birth.[63] Near Hawkshead are the remains of the house, where the Abbot of Furness 'kept residence by one or more monks, who performed divine service and other parochial duties in the neighbourhood.' There is still a court-room over the gateway, 'where the bailiff of Hawkshead held court, and distributed justice, in the name of the abbot.'[64]

From the tremendous steeps of the long fell, which towers over Hawkshead, astonishing views open to the distant vales and mountains of Cumberland; overlooking all the grotesque summits in the neighbourhood of Grasmere, the fells of Borrowdale in the furthest distance, Langdale-pikes, and several small lakes, seen gleaming in the bosom of the mountains. Before us, rose the whole multitude of Coniston-fells, of immense height and threatening forms, their tops thinly darkened with thunder mists, and, on the left, Furness-fells sinking towards the bay, which Ulverston sands form for the sea.

As we advanced, Coniston-fells seemed to multiply, and became still more impressive, till, having reached at length the summit of the mountain, we looked down upon Thurston-lake immediately below, and saw them rising abruptly round its northern end in somewhat of the sublime attitudes and dark majesty of Ullswater. A range of lower rocks, nearer to the eye, exhibited a very peculiar and grotesque appearance, coloured scars and deep channels marking their purple sides, as if they had been rifted by an earthquake.

The road descends the flinty steeps towards the eastern bank of the lake, that spreads a surface of six miles in length and generally three quarters of a mile in breadth, not winding in its course, yet much indented with bays, and presenting nearly its whole extent at once to the eye. The grandest features are the fells, that crown its northern end, not distantly and gradually, like those of Windermere, nor varied like them with magnificent colouring, but rising in haughty abruptness, dark, rugged and stupendous, within a quarter of a mile of the margin, and shutting out all prospect of other mountain-summits. At their feet, pastures spread a bright green to the brim of the lake. Nearly in the centre of these fells, which open in a semicircle to receive the lake, a cataract descends, but its shining line is not of a breadth proportioned to the vastness of its perpendicular fall. The village of Coniston is sweetly seated under shelter of the rocks; and, at a distance beyond, on the edge of the water, the antient hall, or priory, shews its turret and ivyed ruins among old woods.[65] The whole picture is reflected in the liquid mirror below. The gay, convivial chorus, or solemn vesper, that once swelled along the lake from these consecrated walls, and awakened, perhaps, the enthusiasm of the voyager, while evening stole upon the scene, is now contrasted by desolation and profound repose, and, as he glides by, he hears only the dashing of his oars, or the surge beating on the shore.

This lake appeared to us one of the most charming we had seen. From the sublime mountains, which bend round its head, the heights, on either side, decline towards the south into waving hills, that form its shores, and often stretch in long sweeping points into the water, generally covered with tufted wood, but sometimes with the tender verdure of pasturage. The tops of these woods were just embrowned with autumn, and contrasted well with other slopes, rough and heathy, that rose above, or fell beside them to the water's brink, and added force to the colouring, which the reddish tints of decaying fern, the purple bloom of heath, and the bright golden gleams of broom, spread over these elegant banks. Their hues, the graceful undulations of the marginal hills and bays, the richness of the woods, the solemnity of the northern fells and the deep repose, that pervades the scene, where only now and then a white cottage or a farm lurks among the trees, are circumstances, which render Thurston-lake one of the most interesting and, perhaps, the most beautiful of any in the country.

The road undulates over copsy hills, and dips into shallow vallies along the whole of the eastern bank, seldom greatly elevated above the water, or descending to a level with it, but frequently opening to extensive views of its beauties, and again shrouding itself in verdant gloom. The most impressive pictures were formed by the fells, that crowd over the upper end of the lake, and which, viewed from a low station, sometimes appeared nearly to enclose that part of it. The effect was then astonishingly grand, particularly about sun-set, when the clouds, drawing upwards, discovered the utmost summits of these fells, and a tint of dusky blue began to prevail over them, which gradually deepened into night. A line of lower rocks, that extend from these, are, independently of the atmosphere, of a dull purple, and their shaggy forms would appear gigantic in almost any other situation. Even here, they preserve a wild dignity, and their attitudes somewhat resemble those at the entrance of Borrowdale; but they are forgotten, when the eye is lifted to the solemn mountains immediately above. These are rich in slate quarries, and have some copper mines; but the latter were closed, during the civil wars of the last century, having been worked, as we are told in the descriptive language of the miners, from *the day to the evening end*, forty fathom, and to the *morning end* seven score fathom; a figurative style of distinguishing the western and eastern directions of the mine. The lake, towards the lower end, narrows and is adorned by one small island; but here the hills of the eastern shore soar into fells, some barren, craggy and nearly perpendicular, others entirely covered with coppice-wood. Two of these, rising over the road, gave fine relief to each other, the one shewing only precipices of shelving rock, while its rival aspired with woods, that mantled from the base to the summit, consisting chiefly of oak, ash and holly. Not any lake, that we saw, is at present so much embellished with wood as Thurston. All the mountains of *High* and the vallies of *Low Furness* were, indeed, some centuries ago, covered with forests, part of which was called the Forest of Lancaster; and these were of such entangled luxuriance as to be nearly impenetrable in many tracts. Here, wolves, wild boars, and a remarkably large breed of deer, called Seghs, the heads of which have frequently been found buried at a considerable depth in the soil, abounded.[66] So secure an asylum did these animals find in the woods of High Furness, that, even after the low lands were cleared and cultivated, shepherds were necessary to guard the flocks from the ravages of the wolves. Towards the end of the thirteenth century, the upper forests also were nearly destroyed.

In winter, the shepherds used to feed their flocks with the young sprouts of ash and holly, a custom said to be still observed; the sheep coming at the call of the shepherd and assembling round the hollytree to receive from his hand the young shoots cropped for them.* Whenever the woods are felled, which is too frequently done, to supply fuel for the neighbouring furnaces, the holly is still held sacred to the flocks of these mountains.

Soon after passing the island, the road enters the village of Nibthwaite, rich only in situation; for the cottages are miserable. The people seemed to be as ignorant as poor; a young man knew not how far it was to Ulverston, or as he called it Ulson, though it was only five miles.

On the point of a promontory of the opposite shore, embosomed in ancient woods, the chimnies and pointed roof of a gray mansion look out most

---

*   West's 'Antiquities of Furness.'

interestingly. The woods open partially to the north, and admit a view of the *Swiss* scenery at the head of the lake, in its finest position. On the other sides, the oaks so embower the house and spread down the rocks, as scarcely to allow it a glimpse of the water bickering between the dark foliage below.

At Nibthwaite, the lake becomes narrow and gradually decreases, till it terminates at Lowick-bridge, where it glides away in the little river Crake, which descends to Ulverston sands. We stopped upon the bridge to take a last view of the scene; the distant fells were disappearing in twilight, but the gray lake gleamed at their base. From the steeps of a lofty mountain, that rose near us on the right, cattle were slowly descending for the night, winding among the crags, sometimes stopping to crop the heath, or broom, and then disappearing for a moment behind the darker verdure of yews, that grew in knots upon the cliffs.

It was night before we reached Ulverston. The wind sounded mournfully among the hills and we perceived our approach to the sea only by the faint roaring of the tide, till from a brow, whence the hills open on either hand with a grand sweep, we could just discern the gray surface of the sea-bay, at a distance below, and then, by lights that glimmered in the bottom, the town of Ulverston, lying not far from the shore and screened on the north by the heights, from which we were to descend.

Ulverston is a neat but ancient town, the capital and chief port of Furness. The road from it to the majestic ruin of Furness Abbey lies through Low Furness, and loses the general wildness and interest of the country, except where now and then the distant retrospect of the mountains breaks over the tame hills and regular enclosures, that border it.

About a mile and a half on this side of the Abbey, the road passes through Dalton, a very antient little town, once the capital of Low Furness, and rendered so important by its neighbourhood to the Abbey, that Ulverston, the present capital, could not then support the weekly market, for which it had obtained a charter. Dalton, however, sunk with the suppression of its neighbouring patrons, and is now chiefly distinguished by the pleasantness of its situation, to which a church, built on a bold ascent, and the remains of a castle, advantageously placed for the command of the adjoining valley, still attach some degree of dignity. What now exists of the latter is one tower, in a chamber of which the Abbot of Furness held his secular Court; and the chamber was afterwards used as a gaol for debtors, till within these few years, when the dead ruin released the living one. The present church-yard and the scite of this castle are supposed to have been included within the limits of a *castellum,* built by Agricola, of the fosse of which there are still some faint vestiges.[67]

Beneath the brow, on which the church and tower stand, a brook flows through a narrow valley, that winds about a mile and a half to the Abbey. In the way thither we passed the entrance of one of the very rich iron mines, with which the neighbourhood abounds; and the deep red tint of the soil, that overspreads almost the whole country between Ulverston and the monastery, sufficiently indicates the nature of the treasures beneath.

In a close glen, branching from this valley, shrouded by winding banks clumped with old groves of oak and chestnut, we found the magnificent remains of

FURNESS ABBEY

THE DEEP RETIREMENT of its situation, the venerable grandeur of its gothic arches and the luxuriant yet ancient trees, that shadow this forsaken spot, are circumstances of picturesque and, if the expression may be allowed, of sentimental beauty, which fill the mind with solemn yet delightful emotion. This glen is called the Vale of Nightshade, or, more literally from its ancient title Bekangsgill, the 'glen of deadly nightshade,' that plant being abundantly found in the neighbourhood. Its romantic gloom and sequestered privacy particularly adapted it to the austerities of monastic life; and in the most retired part of it King Stephen, while Earl of Mortaign and Bulloign, founded, in the year 1127, the magnificent monastery of Furness, and endowed it with princely wealth and almost princely authority, in which it was second only to Fontain's-abbey in Yorkshire.

North View of Furness Abbey engraved by R. Scott, pub. C. Law, 1800)

The windings of the glen conceal these venerable ruins, till they are closely approached, and the bye road, that conducted us, is margined with a few ancient oaks, which stretch their broad branches entirely across it, and are finely preparatory objects to the scene beyond. A sudden bend in this road brought us within view of the northern gate of the Abbey, a beautiful gothic arch, one side of which is luxuriantly festooned with nightshade. A thick grove of plane-trees, with some oak and beech, overshadow it on the right, and lead the eye onward to the ruins of the Abbey, seen through this dark arch in remote perspective, over rough but verdant ground. The principal features are the great northern window and part of the eastern choir, with glimpses of shattered arches and stately walls beyond, caught between the gaping casements. On the left, the bank of the glen is broken into knolls capped with oaks, which in some places spread downwards to a stream that winds round the ruin, and darken it with their rich foliage. Through this gate is the entrance to the immediate precincts of the Abbey, an area said to contain sixty-five acres, now called the Deer-park. It is enclosed by a stone wall, on which the remains of many small buildings and the faint vestiges of others, still appear; such as the porter's lodge, mills, granaries, ovens and kilns that once supplied the monastery, some of which, seen under the shade of the fine old trees, that on every side adorn the broken steeps of this glen, have a very interesting effect.

Just within the gate, a small manor house of modern date, with its stables and other offices, breaks discordantly upon the lonely grandeur of the scene. Except this, the character of the deserted ruin is scrupulously preserved in the surrounding area; no spade has dared to level the inequalities, which fallen fragments have occasioned in the ground, or shears to clip the wild fern and underwood, that overspread it; but every circumstance conspires to heighten the solitary grace of the principal object and to prolong the luxurious melancholy, which the view of it inspires. We made our way among the pathless fern and grass to the north end of the church, now, like every other part of the Abbey, entirely roofless, but shewing the lofty arch of the great window, where, instead of the painted glass that once enriched it, are now tufted plants and wreaths of nightshade. Below is the principal door of the church, bending into a deep round arch, which, retiring circle within circle, is rich and beautiful; the remains of a winding stair-case are visible within the wall on its left side. Near this northern end of the edifice are seen one side of the eastern choir, with its two slender gothic window frames, and on the west a remnant of the nave of the Abbey and some lofty arches, which once belonged to the belfry, now detached from the main building.

To the south, but concealed from this point of view, are the chapter-house, some years ago exhibiting a roof of beautiful gothic fretwork, and which was almost the only part of the Abbey thus ornamented, its architecture having been characterised by an air of grand simplicity rather than by the elegance and richness of decoration, which in an after date distinguished the gothic style in England. Over the chapter-house were once the library and scriptorium, and beyond it are still the remains of cloisters, of the refectory, the locutorium, or conversation-room, and the calefactory.[68] These, with the walls of some chapels, of the vestry, a hall, and of what is believed to have been a school-house, are all the features of this noble edifice that can easily be traced: winding stair-cases within the surprising thickness of the walls, and door-cases involved in darkness and mystery, the place abounds with.

The abbey, which was formerly of such magnitude as nearly to fill up the breadth of the glen, is built of a pale-red stone, dug from the neighbouring rocks, now changed by time and weather to a tint of dusky brown, which accords well with the hues of plants and shrubs that every where emboss the mouldering arches.

The finest view of the ruin is on the east side, where, beyond the vast, shattered frame that once contained a richly-painted window, is seen a perspective of the choir and of distant arches, remains of the nave of the abbey, closed by the woods. This perspective of the ruin is* said to be two hundred and eighty-seven feet in length; the choir part of it is in width only twenty-eight feet inside, but the nave is seventy: the walls, as they now stand, are fifty-four feet high and in thickness five. Southward from the choir extend the still beautiful, though broken, pillars and arcades of some chapels, now laid open to the day; the chapter-house, the cloisters, and beyond all, and detached from all, is the school-house, a large building, the only part of the monastery that still boasts a roof.

As, soothed by the venerable shades and the view of a more venerable ruin, we rested opposite to the eastern window of the choir, where once the high altar stood, and, with five other altars, assisted the religious pomp of the scene; the images and the manners of times, that were past, rose to reflection. The midnight procession of monks, clothed in white and bearing lighted tapers, appeared to the 'mind's eye' issuing to the choir through the very door-case, by which such processions were wont to pass from the cloisters to perform the matin service, when, at the moment of their entering the church, the deep chanting of voices was heard, and the organ swelled a solemn peal.[69] To fancy,

---

*   'Antiquities of Furness.'

the strain still echoed feebly along the arcades and died in the breeze among the woods, the rustling leaves mingling with the close. It was easy to image the abbot and the officiating priests seated beneath the richly-fretted canopy of the four stalls, that still remain entire in the southern wall, and high over which is now perched a solitary yew-tree, a black funereal memento to the living of those who once sat below.

Of a quadrangular court on the west side of the church, three hundred and thirty-four feet long and one hundred and two feet wide, little vestige now appears, except the foundation of a range of cloisters, that formed its western boundary, and under the shade of which the monks on days of high solemnity passed in their customary procession round the court. What was the belfry is now a huge mass of detached ruin, picturesque from the loftiness of its shattered arches and the high inequalities of the ground within them, where the tower, that once crowned this building, having fallen, lies in vast fragments, now covered with earth and grass, and no longer distinguishable but by the hillock they form.

The school-house, a heavy structure attached to the boundary wall on the south, is nearly entire, and the walls, particularly of the portal, are of enormous thickness, but, here and there, a chasm discloses the stair-cases, that wind within them to chambers above. The schoolroom below, shews only a stone bench, that extends round the walls, and a low stone pillar in the eastern corner, on which the teacher's pulpit was formerly fixed. The lofty vaulted roof is scarcely distinguishable by the dusky light admitted through one or two narrow windows placed high from the ground, perhaps for the purpose of confining the scholar's attention to his book.

These are the principal features, that remain of this once magnificent abbey. It was dedicated to St. Mary, and received a colony of monks from the monastery of Savigny in Normandy, who were called Gray Monks, from their dress of that colour, till they became Cistercians, and, with the severe rules of St. Bernard, adopted a white habit, which they retained till the dissolution of monastic orders in England. The original rules of St. Bernard partook in several instances of the austerities of those of La Trapp, and the society did not very readily relinquish the milder laws of St. Benedict for the new rigours imposed upon them by the parent monastery of Savigny.[70] They were forbidden to taste flesh, except when ill, and even eggs, butter, cheese and milk, but on extraordinary occasions; and denied even the use of linen and fur. The monks were divided into two classes, to which separate departments belonged. Those, who attended the choir, slept upon straw in their usual habits, from which, at midnight, they rose and passed into the church, where they continued their holy hymns, during the short remainder of the night. After this first mass, having publicly confessed themselves, they retired to their cells, and the day was employed in spiritual exercises and in copying or illuminating manuscripts. An unbroken silence was observed, except when, after dinner, they withdrew into the locutorium, where for an hour, perhaps, they were permitted the common privilege of social beings. This class was confined to the boundary wall, except that, on some particular days, the members of it were allowed to walk in parties beyond it, for exercise and amusement; but they were very seldom permitted either to receive, or pay visits. Like the monks of La Trapp, however, they were distinguished for extensive charities and liberal hospitality; for travellers were so scrupulously entertained at the abbey, that it was not till the dissolution that an inn was thought necessary in this part of Furness, when one was opened for their accommodation, expressly because the monastery could no longer receive them.

To the second class were assigned the cultivation of the lands and the performance of domestic affairs in the monastery.

This was the second house in England, that received the Bernardine rules, the most rigorous of which were, however, dispensed with in 1485 by Sixtus the Fourth, when, among other indulgences, the whole order was allowed to taste meat on three days of the week.[71] With the rules of St. Benedict, the monks had exchanged their gray habit for a white cassock with a white caul and scapulary. But their choir dress was either white or gray, with caul and scapulary of the same, and a girdle of black wool; over that a mozet, or hood, and a rochet.* When they went abroad they wore a caul and full black hood.[72]

The privileges and immunities, granted to the Cistercian order in general, were very abundant; and those to the Abbey of Furness were proportioned to its vast endowments. The abbot, it has been mentioned, held his secular court in the neighbouring castle of Dalton, where he presided with the power of administering not only justice but injustice, since the lives and property of the villain tenants of the lordship of Furness were consigned by a grant of King Stephen to the disposal of my lord abbot! The monks also could be arraigned, for whatever crime, only by him. 'The military establishment of Furness likewise depended on the abbot. Every mesne lord and free homager, as well as the customary tenants, took an oath of fealty to the abbot, to be true to him against all men, excepting the king.[73] Every mesne lord obeyed the summons of the abbot, or his steward, in raising his quota of armed men, and every tenant of a whole tenement furnished a man and horse of war for guarding

*   'Antiquities of Furness.'

the coast, for the border-service, or any expedition against the common enemy of the king and kingdom. The habiliments of war were a steel coat, or coat of mail, a falce, or falchion, a jack, the bow, the bill, the cross-bow and spear.[74] The Furness legion consisted of four divisions:—one of bowmen horsed and harnessed; bylmen horsed and harnessed; bowmen without horse and harness; bylmen without horse and harness."[75]

The deep forests, that once surrounded the Abbey, and overspread all Furness, contributed with its insulated situation, on a neck of land running out into the sea, to secure it from the depredations of the Scots, who were continually committing hostilities on the borders. On a summit over the Abbey are the remains of a beacon, or watchtower, raised by the society for their further security. It commands extensive views over Low Furness and the bay of the sea immediately beneath; looking forward to the town and castle of Lancaster, appearing faintly on the opposite coast; on the south, to the isles of Walney, Foulney, and their numerous islets, on one of which stands Peel-castle; and, on the north, to the mountains of High Furness and Coniston, rising in grand amphitheatre round this inlet of the Irish Channel. Description can scarcely suggest the full magnificence of such a prospect, to which the monks, emerging from their concealed cells below, occasionally resorted to sooth the asperities, which the severe discipline of superstition inflicted on the temper; or, freed from the observance of jealous eyes, to indulge, perhaps, the sigh of regret, which a consideration of the world they had renounced, thus gloriously given back to their sight, would sometimes awaken.

From Hawcoat, a few miles to the west of Furness, the view is still more extensive, whence, in a clear day, the whole length of the Isle of Man may be seen, with part of Anglesey and the mountains of Caernarvon, Merionethshire, Denbighshire and Flintshire, shadowing the opposite horizon of the channel.[76]

The sum total of all rents belonging to the Abbey immediately before the dissolution was 946l. 2s. 10d. collected from Lancashire, Cumberland, and even from the Isle of Man; a sum, which considering the value of money at that period; and the woods, meadows, pastures, and fisheries, retained by the society in their own hands; the quantity of provisions for domestic use brought by the tenants instead of rent, and the shares of mines, mills, and saltworks, which belonged to the Abbey, swells its former riches to an enormous amount.

Pyle, the last abbot, surrendered with twenty-nine monks, to Henry the Eighth, April the 9th 1537, and in return was made Rector of Dalton, a situation then valued at thirty-three pounds six shillings and eight-pence a year.

* Ibid.

FROM ULVERSTON TO LANCASTER

FROM THE ABBEY we returned to Ulverston, and from thence crossed
the sands to Lancaster, a ride singularly interesting and sublime. From
the Carter's house, which stands on the edge of the Ulverston sands, and at
the point, whence passengers enter them, to Lancaster, within the furthest
opposite shore, is fifteen miles. This noble bay is interrupted by the peninsula
of Cartmel, extending a line of white rocky coast, that divides the Leven and
Ulverston sands from those of Lancaster. The former are four miles over; the
latter seven.

We took the early part of the tide, and entered these vast and desolate
plains before the sea had entirely left them, or the morning mists were sufficiently
dissipated to allow a view of distant objects; but the grand sweep of the coast
could be faintly traced, on the left, and a vast waste of sand stretching far below
it, with mingled streaks of gray water, that heightened its dreary aspect. The
tide was ebbing fast from our wheels, and its low murmur was interrupted, first,
only by the shrill small cry of sea-gulls, unseen, whose hovering flight could be
traced by the sound, near an island that began to dawn through the mist; and
then, by the hoarser croaking of sea-geese, which took a wider range, for their
shifting voices were heard from various quarters of the surrounding coast. The
body of the sea, on the right, was still involved, and the distant mountains on
our left, that crown the bay, were also viewless; but it was sublimely interesting
to watch the heavy vapours beginning to move, then rolling in lengthening
volumes over the scene, and, as they gradually dissipated, discovering through
their veil the various objects they had concealed—fishermen with carts and
nets stealing along the margin of the tide, little boats putting off from the
shore, and, the view still enlarging as the vapours expanded, the main sea itself
softening into the horizon, with here and there a dim sail moving in the hazy
distance. The wide desolation of the sands, on the left, was animated only
by some horsemen riding remotely in groups towards Lancaster, along the
winding edge of the water, and by a mussel-fisher in his cart trying to ford the
channel we were approaching.

The coast round the bay was now distinctly, though remotely, seen,
rising in woods, white cliffs and cultivated slopes towards the mountains
of Furness, on whose dark brows the vapours hovered. The shore falls into
frequent recesses and juts out in promontories, where villages and country seats
are thickly strewn. Among the latter, Holker-hall, deep among woods, stands
in the north. The village and hall of Bardsea, once the site of a monastery, with
a rocky back-ground and, in front, meadows falling towards the water; and

Conishead priory, with its spiry woods, the paragon of beauty, lie along the western coast, where the hills, swelling gently from the isle of Walney, nearly the last point of land visible on that side the bay, and extending to the north, sweep upwards towards the fells of High Furness and the whole assemblage of Westmoreland mountains, that crown the grand boundary of this arm of the sea.[77]

Lancaster Sands by J. M. W. Turner, c. 1825

We set out rather earlier than was necessary, for the benefit of the guide over part of these trackless wastes, who was going to his station on a sand near the first ford, where he remains to conduct passengers across the united streams of the rivers Crake and Leven, till the returning tide washes him off. He is punctual to the spot as the tides themselves, where he shivers in the dark comfortless midnights of winter, and is scorched on the shadeless sands, under the noons of summer, for a stipend of ten pounds a year! and he said that he had fulfilled the office for thirty years. He has, however, perquisites occasionally from the passengers.[78] In early times the Prior of Conishead, who established the guide, paid him with three acres of land and an annuity of fifteen marks;[79] at the dissolution, Henry the Eighth charged himself and his successors with the payment of the guide by patent.

Near the first ford is Chapel Isle, on the right from Ulverston, a barren sand, where are yet some remains of a chapel, built by the monks of Furness, in which divine service was daily performed at a certain hour, for passengers, who crossed the sands with the morning tide. The ford is not thought dangerous, though the sands frequently shift, for the guide regularly tries for, and ascertains, the proper passage. The stream is broad and of formidable appearance, spreading rapidly among the sands and, when you enter it, seeming to bear you away in its course to the sea. The second ford is beyond the peninsula of Cartmel, on the Lancaster sands, and is formed by the accumulated waters of the rivers, Ken and Winster, where another guide waits to receive the traveller.

The shores of the Lancaster sands fall back to greater distance and are not so bold, or the mountains beyond so awful, as those of Ulverston; but they are various, often beautiful, and Arnside-fells have a higher character. The town and castle of Lancaster, on an eminence, gleaming afar off over the level sands and backed by a dark ridge of rocky heights, look well as you approach them. Thither we returned and concluded a tour, which had afforded infinite delight in the grandeur of its landscapes and a reconciling view of human nature in the simplicity, integrity, and friendly disposition of the inhabitants.

Editorial Notes

The base text for *Observations* is *A Journey Made in the Summer of 1794, through Holland and the Western Frontier of Germany, with a Return down the Rhine: to which are added Observations during a Tour to the Lakes of Lancashire, Westmoreland, and Cumberland* (London: G. G. and J. Robinson, 1795). Only the Lakes section of that full tour is reprinted here. Where references are made to the full tour in the editorial notes this is abbreviated to *Journey* and page numbers to the 1795 edition are given in parenthesis.

This is the first edition of the Lakes section of Radcliffe's 1794 tour to be published separately and in its entirety, thus allowing readers to encounter this distinct and important section of the wider travel guide as a fully autonomous piece of work for the first time.

Original spellings, punctuation, italicization, and capitalization have in most instances been retained. The only corrections made are where there appears to have been a typographical error or where there is a lack of consistency in terms of presentation within the text; in such instances the mistake has been silently corrected.

The reader encounters many archaic and unfamiliar spellings of place names within *Observations* as in other early travel guides. These have been retained in order to provide a more authentic sense of the still relative unfamiliarity and topographical newness of the area. In identifying specific fells and locations within her tour Radcliffe draws on both earlier written guides and on local knowledge and terminology; she records at one point for example that 'A shepherd boy told us the names of almost all of the heights within the horizon'. She goes on to admit to her 'uncertainty as to the titles of heights; for the people of each village have a name for the part of the mountain nearest to themselves, and they sometimes call the whole by that name.' Later she notes that not 'only every fell of this wild region has a name, but almost every crag of every fell.' One consequence of hearing rather than reading some place names and of gleaning local names for specific parts of a fell, combined with the strong dialect in which such details were probably imparted, is that there are occasionally issues with the accurate identification of numerous place-references in Radcliffe's text. Many of the names she uses are clearly phonetic renderings of what she has heard and while in most cases the modern reader can translate these fairly easily (e.g. 'Kidstowpike' clearly refers to 'Kidsty Pike') on some occasions it is less easy to identify references to names which may have passed out of use or which are remembered only as local pockets of knowledge. To reference all of the allusions to crags and fells listed in the text would have a very disruptive effect on the reading experience, so the editorial notes are confined to offering commentary or information on details such as literary quotations, individuals mentioned by name, gentlemen's residences, archaic or specialist terminology, and other specific points of interest.

Radcliffe added a small number of footnotes and these have been retained and are presented as footnotes within the main text.

Notes

1 Having landed back in England Radcliffe describes journeying northwards from London, pausing only briefly to explore the Elizabethan Hardwick Hall in Derbyshire, then passing onwards through Stockport and Manchester, 'a second London' (*Journey*, p. 377), before heading to Lancaster.

2 *the Rheingau:* district in which the Rhine is situated. The area reaches down on the Northern side of the river Rhine between the German towns of Wiesbaden and Lorch.
   Mentz: archaic English name for Mainz – the capital of what is now the state of Rhineland-Palatinate in Germany.

3 The poet Thomas Gray visited the Lakes in 1769 and an account of his visit was published in 1775. Gray's *Journal* rapidly became one of the most influential of the contemporary travel guides and is the text also prioritised by Charlotte Smith in her 1789 Grasmere-based novel, *Ethelinde; or, the Recluse of the Lake* and by Wordsworth in his *Guide to the Lakes* (1835).

4 Radcliffe misquotes from Anna Letitia Barbauld's poem 'The Invitation' (1772); the line should actually read 'And drink the spirit of the mountain breeze'. *The Poems of Anna Letitia Barbauld*, ed. William McCarthy and Elizabeth Kraft (Athens and London: University of Georgia Press, 1994), p. 10. l. 18.

5 There are a number of motte-and-bailey and other castles from the Norman period within the Lune Valley but none listed with this name. Radcliffe may be referring to 'Thurland Castle' which was left in ruins following an attack during the Civil

War; the ruins were subsequently bought and converted into a country house in 1810.

6 Thomas Fenwick (c. 1729-1794) was MP for Westmorland (1768-74). The name of the mansion itself was actually Burrow Hall not Overborough and this still stands in Burrow-with-Burrow, near Kirkby Londsdale. Overborough is an archaic name for Burrow itself and was once the site of a Roman fort.

7 Kirkby Londsale Bridge is now more commonly known as 'Devil's Bridge'. West describes it as 'more venerable than handsome'. Thomas West, *A Guide to the Lakes*, 4th edn. (London: Richardson *et al*, 1789), p. 173.

8 A debate about the Roman settlement at Kendal occurs in older sources, such as William Camden's *Britannia* of 1586, and in more contemporaneous texts, including Robert Henry's *The History of Britain;* Henry suggests that the identification of the Roman fort at Kendal was a mistake. *The History of Britain, from the First Invasion of it by the Romans under Julius Cæsar,* 2 vols (London: Strahan and Cadell, 1788), II, (p. 420). All of these sources refer though to the fort in question by the name of 'Brovonacæ' not 'Brocanonacio', which suggests that Radcliffe's spelling of the name of the fort is inaccurate. West is unlikely to be an important source here as he alludes only in vague terms to Kendal castle 'probably' having been built 'on the ruins of a Roman station' (West, *Guide*, p. 178).

9 Kendal Green was a coarse cloth traditionally worn by the rural lower-classes. Falstaff refers to having been attacked by 'three misbegotten knaves in Kendal green'. *Henry IV, P1:* Act II, Scene 4, ll. 216-7.

10 Further historical details about these families are provided in West's *Guide*, pp. 175-6.

11 The Bellingham family motto translates as 'Thus it is'.

12 The obelisk is built on Castle Howe and the plaque reads: 'Sacred to liberty. This Obelisk was erected in the year 1788 in memory of the revolution on 1688'. The monument was built by Kendal stone mason, William Holme, to a design by Francis Webster.

13 Line taken from James Beattie's poem, *The Minstrel; or, The Progress of Genius* (1771/2). *The Poetical Works of James Beattie* (Boston: Osgood, 1871), p. 37, l. 54.

14 Ossian is the supposed ancient Scottish author of a cycle of epic poems. The poems were presented as translations from ancient sources by the Scottish poet James Macpherson from 1760, coming out as the collected edition, *The Works of Ossian*, in 1765. The poems achieved widespread popularity in the Romantic period and have been described as a 'brooding and potent force in the topography of [Radcliffe's] imagination'. Bonamy Dobrée, 'Explanatory Notes', in *The Mysteries of Udolpho by Ann Radcliffe* (Oxford: Oxford University Press, 1980), p. 674.

15 *As You Like It*: Act II, Scene 7, l. 114.

16 Edmund Gibson (1669-1748) served as Bishop of Lincoln and Bishop of London.

17 John Law (1745–1810) was a Cambridge mathematician and clergyman. He subsequently became a bishop in the Church of Ireland.

18 See note 46 in the main Introduction. The Old Vicarage, Martindale (now a Grade II listed building) does not in any case fit with this description; it is located near Ullswater not Haweswater and is positioned at too great a distance from the lake

to match Radcliffe's account of the garden 'falling towards the water'. The most likely explanation therefore is that Radcliffe is actually describing the village of Mardale which was destroyed in the 1930s following the damming of Haweswater. An impressive parsonage was built in Mardale in 1858 at the foot of Castle Crag but a curacy was in place for Mardale chapel since 1728 and Radcliffe is probably therefore referring to an earlier residence which was used as a parsonage prior to the building of the later Victorian property.

19 If the supposition proposed in the note above is correct, Radcliffe is referring here to Holy Trinity Church, a tiny post-reformation chapel which was destroyed during the damming of the lake.

20 Given James Plumptre's satirical portrait of Veronica, his Gothic novelist in *The Lakers* (1798), it is interesting that Radcliffe does not actually display any pseudo-botanical knowledge during her tour. See the main Introduction for further discussion of Plumptre's text.

21 Thomas Gray refers to both Dalemain and Hutton St. John. Dalemain House had been owned by the Hassel family since 1680 and is now open to the public. Dalemain is described by Gray as a large fabrick of pale red stone' and Hutton St. John as the 'castle-like old mansion of Mr Huddleston'. Gray also misspells both the houses and owners' names but his misspellings are slightly different to those of Radcliffe. *Thomas Gray's Journal of his Visit to the Lake District in October 1769*, ed. William Roberts (Liverpool: Liverpool University Press), p. 33.

22 Radcliffe misquotes again here, this time from a line spoken by Hippolyta in *A Midsummer Night's Dream* which actually reads: 'as imagination bodies forth / The form of things unknown'. *A Midsummer Night's Dream*: Act V, Scene 1, ll. 15-16.

23 These details are probably derived from James Clarke's, *A Survey of the Lakes of Cumberland, Westmorland, and Lancashire* (London: Robson and Faulder, 1787), p. 25, who records almost the same information.

24 Colonel John Robinson was Sheriff of Cumberland from 1769-1770. He died in 1807. His impressive property appears on the far right in a painting by Joseph Farrington, entitled 'View from Watermillock and the Lower end of Ullswater' which was published as an engraving in *Views of the Lakes etc. in Cumberland and Westmorland* (1789).

25 Charles Howard (1746 –1815) was the 11th Duke of Norfolk. Lyulph's Tower is described by Lindop as a 'Gothic hunting lodge built by the Duke of Norfolk in 1780'. He notes that the tower would appear in Walter Scott's *The Bridal of Triermain* (1805). Though the tower was merely pseudo-Gothic, Scott too recognised the more archaic potential of the landscape in which it was set. In his poem Sir Roland de Vaux travels to the tower to seek the advice of a chieftain 'Lyulph' who 'Gifted like his gifted race / He the characters can trace, / Graven deep in elder time / Upon Helvellyn's cliffs sublime'. Grevel Lindop, *A Literary Guide to the Lake District* (Wilmslow: Sigma Press, 2005), p. 267.

26 John Mounsey (1758-1821) and his wife Mary lived at Patterdale Hall. Dorothy Wordsworth, in her journal entry for 22 December 1801 gives a little insight into life at the Hall, noting that 'When we were at Thomas Ashburner's on Sunday Peggy talked about the Queen of Patterdale. She had been brought to drinking by her husband's unkindness and avarice. She was formerly a very nice tidy woman.

She had taken to drinking but "that was better than if she had taken to something worse" (by this I suppose she meant killing herself). She said that her husband used to be out all night with other women & she used to *hear* him come in the morning, for they never slept together.' Dorothy Wordsworth, *The Grasmere and Alfoxden Journals* (Oxford: Oxford UP, 2002), p. 52. Southey later refers to the 'detestable house here belonging to a gentleman, who for his great possessions in the vale is called the King of Paterdale' *[sic]*. Robert Southey, *Letters from England: by Don Manuel Alvarez Espriella,* 3 vols (London: Longman, 1808), II, p. 143.

27 West's 3ʳᵈ station was positioned above the King's Arms Inn at Patterdale (now the Patterdale Hotel). West writes 'There is from the top of the rock, above the inn, a very charming view of the last bend of the lake, which constitutes one of the finest landscapes on it, and takes in just enough for a delightful picture. The nearest fore-ground is a fall of inclosures. A rocky wooded mountain that hangs over *Patterdale-house* (called *Martindale-fell*) is in a proper point of distance to the right. Steep rocks, and shaggy woods hanging from their sides, are on the left. *Gowbarrow-park* rises in a fine style from the water edge for the back-ground, and a noble reach of water, beautifully spotted with rocky isles, charmingly disposed, with perpetual change of rocky shore, fill the middle space of this beautiful picture' (West, *Guide*, p. 154).

    Beau idée: Reynolds actually refers to the *beau ideal*, meaning the ideal beauty. See Discourse III – Sir Joshua Reynolds, *Discourses on Art*, ed. Robert R. Wark (New Haven and London: Yale UP, 1997).

28 *Berg strasse:* mountain road.

29 These lines are taken from 'The Songs of Selna'. *Fingal, an Ancient Poem, in Six Books: Together with several other Poems, composed by Ossian the Son of Fingal,* trans. James Macpherson (London: Becket and De Hondt, 1762), p. 217.

30 *Juvenal:* Decimus Iunius Iuvenalis, known in English as Juvenal. Roman poet active in the late first and early second century AD, originator of the genre of the satire and author of the *Satires*.

31 The lines are taken from the second book of *De Rerum Natura* [*The Nature of Things*], a poem in six books by the Roman poet and philosopher Lucretius (c. 99 BC – c. 55 BC) and translate as: 'It is sweet, when the winds disturb the waters on the vast deep, to behold from the land the great distress of another'. The text goes on 'not because it is a joyous pleasure that anyone should be-made-to-suffer, but because it is agreeable to see from what evils thou art free'. *Lucretius: On the Nature of Things,* Trans. John Selby Watson (London: Henry Bohn, 1851), p. 54.

32 The lines are taken from 'Winter' in James Thomson's, *The Seasons* [1726]. The full passage reads:

> Now, all amid the rigours of the year,
> In the wild depth of Winter, while without
> The ceaseless winds blow ice, be my retreat,
> Between the groaning forest and the shore,
> Beat by a boundless multitude of waves,
> A rural, shelter'd, solitary, scene;
> Where ruddy fire and beaming tapers join,
> To chase the cheerless gloom. There let me sit,

And hold high converse with the mighty dead[.]

The Poetical Works of James Thomson (London and Edinburgh: Nimmo, 1878), p. 169, ll. 413-422.

33 Carleton Hall is now the Headquarters for Cumbria Police; Thomas Wallace (1768-1844) was an MP.

34 Lindop notes that this is a mistake which originated from James Clarke's *Survey of the Lakes* (1787), and claims that in fact 'Sidney was never at Brougham' (Lindop, p. 110). It was clearly a popular idea in Romantic contexts though and such literary antecedents would no doubt have appealed to the writers who came to the region. Wordsworth too pauses over the literary connection in *The Prelude*:

> A mansion not unvisited of old
>
> By Sidney, where, in sight of our Helvellyn,
>
> Some snatches he might pen, for aught we know,
>
> Of his Arcadia.

William Wordsworth, *The Major Works*, ed. Stephen Gill (Oxford: Oxford University Press, 2008), p. 456, ll. 222-225).

35 West identifies Brougham as the '*Brovoniacum* of the *Romans*' (West, *Guide*, p. 167).

36 Radcliffe's main source for these details is probably Clarke's *Survey* (1787) which offers similar information (see Clarke, p. 4).

Vipont: the family name is usually spelt 'Vieuxpont'.

37 *fulling-mills:* mills at which cloth was beaten and cleaned in water, thus shrinking the fibres of the cloth and producing a denser fabric.

38 Hardwick Hall in Derbyshire which the Radcliffes had visited on their journey North.

39 The Le Flemings had been an important family in the region since the original Michael Le Fleming came over with William the Conqueror in the 12th century and was granted lands in Cumberland.

40 The line is taken from John Milton's, 'L'Allegro'. *Milton: Poetical Works,* ed. Douglas Bush (London: Oxford University Press, 1966), p. 90, l. 78.

41 Wordsworth would later also celebrate this monument and the 'bright flower of Charity' in a sonnet published in 1835 entitled 'Countess' Pillar'. *The Poetical Works of Wordsworth*, ed. Thomas Hutchinson (London: Oxford University Press, 1953), p. 310, l. 2.

42 Gray notes having dined with the landlady, Mrs Buchanan, at three o'clock in the afternoon, on 'trout and partridge' (*Gray's Journal*, p. 27).

43 Richard Burn (1709-1785), a Westmorland-born doctor of law and antiquarian. He collaborated with Joseph Nicholson to produce *The History and Antiquities of the Counties of Westmorland and Cumberland*, 2 vols (London: Cadell, 1777).

44 '*Hot trod* was the pursuit of offenders, called moss-troopers, by blood-hounds, or *slough dogs*, as they were named'. John Britton and Edward Wedlake Brayley, *The Beauties of England and Wales; or, Delineations, Topographical, Historical, and Descriptive of Each County*, 18 vols (London: Vernor and Hood *et al*, 1802), III, p. 13.

45 *Tacitus:* Roman senator and historian. The lines are taken from *The Germania* 36:1: 'When force decides everything, forbearance and righteousness are qualities

attributed only to the strong'. *Tacitus: The Agricola and the Germania*, trans. H. Mattingly (London: Penguin, 1970), p. 131. There is, however, some scholarly debate about the precise translation of these lines and thus the exact nature of the 'reproof' being offered – see Kenneth Wellesley, 'Tacitus. *Germania* 36.1', *The Classical Quarterly* 20:2 (1970), 371-371.

46 The lines are taken from Milton's 'Comus'. *Poetical Works*, p. 116, l. 89 and p. 126, l. 500.

47 *flagitious:* criminal; villainous.

48 The lines are taken from William Mason's dramatic poem, *Caractacus* (1759). *Caractacus, A Dramatic Poem: Written on the Model of the Ancient Greek Tragedy* (London: Knapton *et al*, 1759), pp. 3-4. The title character is a British chieftain supposed to have led resistance to Roman conquest.

49 In 1778 Joseph Pocklington bought Derwent Island (then known as Vicar's Island) and built there a house, boathouse, fort and battery, and Druid circle. These were later removed by a subsequent owner and just over a decade later, in his *Letters from England,* Southey would observe that 'A few years ago' the island 'was hideously disfigured with forts and batteries, a sham church, and a new druidical temple.... The present owner has done all which a man of taste could do in removing these deformities' (Southey, p. 153).

twelfthcake: a Twelfth Cake was a decorated cake produced to mark the festival of Epiphany in the eighteenth-century; it was usually elaborately adorned with crowns and other decorations.

50 This extended engagement with Milton's 'Comus' is interesting and is discussed in the main Introduction. The plot of Milton's verse-drama involves a young woman being captured by the necromancer, Comus, whilst abandoned in a dark wood. Her brothers have gone off in search of sustenance for her and while they are absent she is tricked by Comus and taken to his palace, where he uses his powers to try to tempt her. Milton's plot therefore shares a number of features with the plots of Radcliffe's own fiction and in quoting so extensively from this text Radcliffe effectively presents the landscape with its 'wildness, seclusion, and magical beauty' as the kind of Gothic landscape of her own fictions. Radcliffe's choice of quotations from the poem emphasises the supernatural, exciting, and magical potential of this landscape. Milton, *Poetical Works*, p. 119, ll. 188-90; p. 126, l. 523; p. 118, ll. 154-6; p. 126, ll. 515-7; p. 118, ll. 171-2; and p. 120, ll. 260-1.

51 Rawnsley describes this as 'apparently, the first ascent, by womankind, of our tremendous mountain' and satirises her 'account of the terrible danger' afforded by the ascent. H. D. Rawnsley, *Literary Associations of the English Lakes,* 2 vols (MacLehose: Glasgow, 1894), I, p. 160. Southey may have had Radcliffe's account in mind when he observes in his own insistently calm ascent of Skiddaw in *Letters from England,* that the route was 'perfectly safe' and constitutes in many places 'easy travelling over turf and moss' (Southey, pp. 156- 157).

52 Ormathwaite Hall, a Grade II listed Georgian mansion house near Keswick was owned by William Brownrigg (1711-1800). Brownrigg was a doctor, eminent scientist, and fellow of the Royal Society who practiced medicine at Whitehaven for 30 years and became known for his work with salt and with mining gases.

During his retirement he encouraged Thomas West to write his *Guide to the Lakes*.

53 *German Ocean:* an earlier name for the North Sea.

54 Radcliffe is misquoting Gray, who writes in his 'jaws of *Borodale*' passage of the 'turbulent Chaos of mountain behind mountain' (*Gray's Journal*, p. 45).

55 *Coriolanus:* Act III, Scene 2, ll. 4-5.

56 *Armithwaite-house:* now Armathwaite Hall Country House and Spa.

57 Gray records that the local farmers would be lowered on ropes to plunder the nests; they would remove both eaglets and eggs in order to reduce the eagle population and thus minimise eagle attacks on lambs and other animals (*Gray's Journal*, p. 47).

58 *jaws of this pass:* Radcliffe's phrase is clearly influenced by Gray's famous description of the 'jaws of *Borodale*' (*Gray's Journal*, p. 45).

59 Wadd or Wad is an early name for Black Lead or Graphite. These mines were already ancient by the date of Radcliffe's tour and had been described as 'famous' in Camden's *Britannia*.

60 Rt Rev Richard Watson (1737–1816) was an Anglican clergyman and academic, who served as the Bishop of Llandaff from 1782 to 1816. He was Cumbrian by birth and purchased the Calgarth estate (which Radcliffe erroneously refers to as 'Culgarth') at Windermere in 1788. He was known for his contributions to the Revolutionary debates of the period and Wordsworth subsequently wrote a pamphlet in 1793 entitled, *Letter to the Bishop of Llandaff*, which was a response to Watson's own defence of the French monarchy.

61 '*fine phrensy*': *A Midsummer Night's Dream:* Act V, Scene 1, l. 12.

62 Thurston-Lake or Thurstonmere was the former name for Coniston Water and was still widely used in the late eighteenth-century.

63 Edwin Sandys, Archbishop of York (1519-1588) founded Hawkshead Grammar School in 1585. This was of course the school at which the young Wordsworth was educated from 1779-1787. Sandys was born in 1519 at Esthwaite Hall, which is one mile south of Hawkshead on the road to Newby Bridge.

64 Radcliffe is citing from West's *Antiquities* [1774]. Thomas West, *The Antiquities of Furness* (London: Ashburner, 1805), p. 32.

65 In his unpublished *Tour* of 1811/12 Wordsworth notes that 'Conistone Hall is 'an ancient half-ruined seat of the Flemings. Its ancient architecture, its dignity & importance as a feudal head to the surrounding Cottages of the Yeomanry would have recommended it to his notice if the building had [remained] undecayed, but nature has beautified the walls & roof with weeds & large masses of ivy, as if to make amends for the injuries of time.' He notes that the 'Traveller must condescend to pay particular' attention to this relatively humble edifice as it is 'with the exception of a few of the village Churches....the most interesting piece of Architecture these Lakes have to boast of'. *The Prose Works of William Wordsworth*, 3 vols, ed. W. J. B. Owen and Jane Worthington Smyser (Clarendon Press, Oxford:1974), II, pp. 306-7.

66 *Seghs:* a gaelic term for a species of large wild deer. West notes in *Antiquities* that an area of High Furness was 'noted for a breed of large deer or seghs' (p. 41). In the base text for *Observations* the deer are actually referred to as 'Leghs' and this error has been corrected in the text as presented here.

67 *Castellum:* a small, isolated Roman fortress; *Agricola:* Gnaeus Julius Agricola (40–

93AD) was a Roman general who, in his role as governor of Britain, conquered large areas of northern England, Scotland and Wales. The biography of Agricola by his son-in-law Tacitus, provides substantial details of his life and campaigns.

fosse: a long, narrow trench or excavation especially in a fortification.

In her account of Dalton castle it seems likely that Radcliffe is drawing on details supplied by Tacitus in *The Agricola* since she reinforces his claim that the castellum was built by Agricola. West also offers an extended discussion of Agricola's presence in Dalton but is more vague as to whether 'he, or some successor' built the castellum (West, *Antiquities*, p. 10).

68 *locutorium:* room in which monks were allowed to converse; *calefactory:* a heated sitting room.

69 '*mind's eye':* Hamlet: Act I, Scene 2, l. 185.

70 *La Trapp:* La Trappe Abbey is a monastery in Normandy which was unified with the older monastery at Savigny Abbey in 1147. La Trappe houses the original Order of Cistercians of the Strict Observance.

71 *Sixtus the Fourth:* Pope Sixtus IV (1414 –1484) for whom the Sistine Chapel was built.

72 *cassock:* full length garment worn by monks and clergy; *caul:* a close-fitting indoor headdress but Radcliffe may mean 'cowl', the hood worn by medieval monks; *scapulary:* Radcliffe probably means 'scapular' – a long wide piece of woollen cloth worn over the shoulders with an opening for the head; *mozet:* (usually mozetta) a short cape with a hood; *rochet:* a garment similar to a surplice.

73 *mesne lord:* a lord holding an estate from a superior feudal lord; *free homager:* a vassal or holder of land by feudal tenure.

74 *a falce, or falchion:* a broad curved sword with a convex edge; *a jack:* a padded tunic; *the bill:* the stick carried by the bylmen (see note 75).

75 *bylmen:* term in the medieval military for men armed with a pointed stick with a hook on the end, used to unseat riders.

76 Radcliffe lists four of the thirteen historic counties of Wales.

77 Radcliffe gives an account of leaving the region by crossing the sands while Wordsworth famously describes entering the region in this way, but both depict this as a liminal space from where the eye is drawn to the mountains which rise up from its edges. As Radcliffe, looking back, sees the 'whole assemblage of Westmorland mountains, that crown the grand boundary of this arm of the sea', so Wordsworth 15 years later would describe the traveller beholding 'rising apparently from its base, the cluster of mountains among which he is going to wander'. William Wordsworth, *Guide to the Lakes*, ed. Ernest de Sélincourt (London: Frances Lincoln, 2004), p. 32.

78 *perquisites:* profits or earnings in addition to main income.

79 *fifteen marks:* the mark was not a coin in English currency and refers rather to a denomination of weight for gold and silver.

INDEX

Note: Places are in or close to the Lake District unless identified otherwise.

TRAVEL LITERATURE FROM HOBNOB PRESS

John Leland Itinerary: a Version in Modern English edited by John Chandler
John Leland's Itinerary is one of the key documents of English local history, offering eye-witness descriptions of hundreds of towns and villages, castles, monasteries and gentry houses during the reign of Henry VIII, by one of the most intelligent and learned observers of his era. John Chandler's modern English version, first published in 1993, identified place and personal names, and rearranged everything of topographical interest into historic English counties, with maps and a detailed introduction. For this new edition he has added parts of the material relating to Leland's travels in Wales, revised the introduction, and established a reliable chronology for the surviving accounts of five journeys which Leland undertook between 1538 and 1544. April 2022, liv, 529pp, maps, paperback, £25.00, ISBN 978-1-914407-29-1

John Taylor, Travels and Travelling, 1616-1653, edited by John Chandler
Taylor (1578-1653), known as the 'Water-Poet', wrote some two hundred pamphlets on every conceivable subject of interest to his contemporaries. His descriptions of the fourteen journeys he made between 1616 and 1653 around Britain (and twice to the continent), are not only entertaining to read, but an important source for anyone interested in travel, places and society before, during and just after the Civil Wars. This expanded edition of a work first published in 1999 includes the two foreign adventures and pamphlets describing carriers, coaches, inns and taverns. October 2020, 512pp, paperback, £18.95, ISBN 978-1-906978-91-4.

The Grand Tour Diaries of William Guise, from Lausanne to Rome edited by Paul and Jane Butler
William, later Sir William, Guise, travelled in Switzerland and Italy in 1764 in the company of Edward Gibbon, the historian. Two journals chronicling in great detail the first part of their tour, from Lausanne to Florence, Rome and other Italian cities, and the cultural sites and artefacts that they saw, have survived in the archives of the family home, Elmore Court in Gloucestershire. There has until now been no full transcription of these journals, which illustrate the historic and cultural interest of two serious Grand Tourists. March 2022, xviii, 190pp, illustrated (some colour) hardback, £25.00, ISBN 978-1-914407-30-7

Journeys in Industrious England, by Thomas Baskerville, edited by Anthea Jones
Except to a very few scholars the name of Thomas Baskerville (1630-1700) is entirely unknown. And yet, like his celebrated younger contemporary, Celia Fiennes, he rode hundreds of miles across many English counties in the later seventeenth century, and recorded in colourful detail where he went and what he observed. Ten journeys and some shorter expeditions were written up, but not published, even in part, for 200 years. His other writings were varied in style and subject matter, including rivers, Oxford colleges, Civil War executions, his own family, and London taverns. This book is a fascinating account of England seen through the eyes of an alert and cheerful man in the late 17th century. October 2023, x, 316pp, paperback, £20.00, ISBN 978-1-914407-51-2

Stage Coaches Explained, the Bristol Example, by Dorian Gerhold
Groundbreaking study of all aspects of coaching between Bristol, Bath and London, and Bristol and other destinations, by the acknowledged authority on pre-railway road transport. A scholarly but readable treatment which penetrates the romantic veneer to provide the key to understanding the stagecoach system as a whole. October 2012, 326 pages, illustrations, maps and tables, paperback, £17.95, ISBN 978-1-906978-15-0 (originally titled *Bristol's Stage Coaches*).

For full details of all **HOBNOB PRESS** titles and ordering information please visit **www.hobnobpress.co.uk**